AS
Travel&Tourism

AS
Travel&Tourism

Philip Allan Updates
Market Place, Deddington, Oxfordshire, OX15 0SE

Orders
Bookpoint Ltd, 130 Milton Park, Abingdon, Oxfordshire, OX14 4SB
tel: 01235 827720
fax: 01235 400454
e-mail: uk.orders@bookpoint.co.uk
Lines are open 9.00 a.m.–5.00 p.m., Monday to Saturday, with a 24-hour
message answering service. You can also order through the Philip Allan
Updates website: www.philipallan.co.uk

© Philip Allan Updates 2005

ISBN-10: 1-84489-407-X
ISBN-13: 978-1-84489-407-9

All efforts have been made to trace copyright on items used.

Author's acknowledgements
Thanks as always to Debbie and Katie for inexhaustible patience and support,
to Philip Cross and all at Philip Allan, and to Bob Holland for the inspiration
to follow the tourism way. I am also grateful to Frédéric Limousin of the
Novotel York for his valuable assistance in researching customer service
staff training.

Printed in Great Britain by CPI Bath

Environmental information
The paper on which this title is printed is sourced from managed,
sustainable forests.

Contents

Introduction

This textbook has been written to support your learning of travel and tourism in the three compulsory units that make up the AS Travel and Tourism single award qualification. It provides comprehensive coverage of their content as laid down by the AQA, Edexcel and OCR specifications. The *AS Travel and Tourism Student Workbook*, also published by Philip Allan, accompanies this textbook.

Course structure

Unit 1 is an externally assessed unit (it has an examination), but Units 2 and 3 are both portfolio (coursework) units for which you need to produce your own work as evidence of your achievements.

In this textbook, Topic 1 provides the key knowledge and understanding needed for the examination, as well as helping to build the appropriate skills such as analysis and evaluation. Topics 2 and 3 cover coursework and are intended to assess your learning of the relevant study areas. This textbook provides the information you will need to help you build the knowledge, understanding and skills necessary to complete your coursework.

Assessment objectives

Throughout your work for all three units, you will acquire knowledge, understanding and skills (including research, analysis and evaluation). You will be assessed against four assessment objectives (AOs):
- demonstration of knowledge, understanding and skills (AO1)
- application of knowledge, understanding and skills (AO2)
- research and analysis (AO3)
- evaluation (AO4)

This book provides material from which you can learn, so that you can demonstrate the use of the four assessment objectives in both the examination and your coursework.

Special features of this book

Starters

Each topic opens with a short Starter chapter. In the case of Topic 1, the Starter poses the key question for you to answer to define the basis of the subject — what exactly is travel and tourism? In Topic 2, the Starter introduces customer service and asserts its key importance to travel and tourism — the people industry. The Starter for Topic 3 presents the world of travel destinations available to customers of the UK travel and tourism industry.

Case studies

Real travel and tourism organisations and real destinations are the subjects of case studies that help build your knowledge and understanding of the travel and tourism industry. All of the case studies are up to date at the time of publication.

Case studies are essential learning for the examination and provide a basis from which you can launch your own investigations for the two coursework units. It is essential that you have a good grasp of a topic before beginning to investigate and assemble your own portfolios.

The range of case studies in this book is wide. They include information on travel and tourism organisations from the major players, such as Thomson, Thomas Cook, easyJet and Novotel to the small- to medium-sized enterprises that are so important to the travel and tourism industry, such as the Village Holidays case study on pages 75–81. Destinations that appeal to domestic, inbound and outbound tourists in the UK, Europe and wider world, including the USA, are also showcased.

Discussion points

In the real world of the travel and tourism industry, issues abound. Change is a constant but can have uncertain outcomes and is viewed differently by different stakeholders. This book signposts potential discussion points as they arise, often in association with case-study material. Discussion points provide focus for class debates, small group discussions or dialogue in pairs.

Support your learning

Support your learning is a collection of practical support tips and tasks that closes each chapter of this textbook under the following headings.

■ **Information sources:** this book is a key information source, but the world of travel and tourism is fast moving so the study of the travel and tourism industry requires you to exploit a range of information sources.

Each chapter presents some key information source suggestions for you or your teacher to access.

- **Skills builder:** each chapter supports skills building and identifies a key skill-building opportunity arising from your learning of that topic. Skills of research, analysis and evaluation are developed through all three units and build as study proceeds. Information selection, editing and written communication are further building blocks. Dealing with people, working as a team and problem solving are skills from the workplace that Topic 2 in particular helps to build. Key skills, including communication, ICT and number, are supported.
- **Activities menu:** at the end of each chapter there is a menu of four activities from which you and your teacher can make selections. Each item on the menu is an activity to support a particular assessment objective — one activity per assessment objective, in numerical order, so Activity 1 is for AO1, Activity 2 is for AO2, and so on. AS Travel and Tourism is a course with a vocational emphasis. It is about an industry in which people apply the knowledge, understanding and skills that you are learning. The activities menus therefore sometimes feature vocational scenarios — settings from the world of the travel and tourism industry from which activities emerge as tasks with real-world application.

Practical scenarios

These feature in each topic. They are extended practical activities, which guide you to research real travel and tourism industry organisations and places, which build learning for the examination and which act as platforms underpinning more detailed research for your coursework units. In Topics 2 and 3, the practical scenarios are initial activities that build knowledge, understanding and skills before you embark on your own independent research.

Course advice

General advice

- Keep up to date. There are two dimensions to this:
  - **Your own work:** the AS course does not take long. Starting in the autumn, you will complete the qualification by the next May or June. There is a lot to learn and do in that time, so it is important from the start to stay on schedule with tasks you are set, with your own reading and with your coursework. Make a written or electronic schedule and monitor yourself. If minor deviations occur, you can reschedule, but try not to fall a long way behind. If there is a problem, ask your teacher for advice.

— **The changing world of travel and tourism:** this book is as up to date as possible. However, the travel and tourism industry and the real world in which it operates are constantly changing. Use the print and broadcast media, including specialist travel press such as *Travel Weekly* and the *Travel Trade Gazette*, to keep up to date. Other information sources, including websites, are suggested in each chapter as tools to help you.

■ Read this book selectively and in bite-size chunks to support your learning in tandem with the teaching you receive. Be aware of the teaching programme and try to read a section ahead of it, reviewing each section after you have been taught it and coming back to it as part of your revision.

■ Know and understand the case studies. For the examination, these provide valuable knowledge that you can use to help you score more marks. For Units 2 and 3 the case studies provide you with important insights you can apply to your investigations.

■ Practise and develop your skills, including analysis and evaluation. In the activities menu at the end of each chapter, Activities 3 and 4 provide you with appropriate opportunities. Higher-level skills score higher marks, and, in any case, analysis of research and evaluation are two specific skills that are assessed in each of the three units of AS Travel and Tourism.

Examination advice

■ Read each question carefully. Every word will have been chosen intentionally by the examiner, so make sure you read and consider the meaning of every word. Focus on the key words.

■ Obey the command words. Each command requires a specific type of response. Some of the common words are as follows:

— **Analyse:** show you understand a set of statistics or interrelationships in depth by using sentences to break down a subject into its essential elements and explain their links and causes. Come to a conclusion.

— **Assess:** say how much or how little — for example, how much effect you expect something to have.

— **Compare and contrast:** compare means to describe the similarities and differences; contrast means to emphasise what the differences are.

— **Define:** use a sentence to give an exact and concise meaning.

— **Describe:** write an account of the main features of something in a little more detail using adjectives. There is no need to explain.

— **Evaluate:** weigh up the point, giving strengths and weaknesses. Write sentences to assess extent (how much?), likelihood (what are the chances of?) or significance (how important?).

- **Explain:** use sentences to clarify why something is as it is, using linking words like 'because' and 'so'.
- **Justify:** use sentences to make clear the reasons behind a decision you have reached or a recommendation you have made.
- **Name:** write what something, someone or somewhere is called. Often, a single word or two is all that is needed. 'Identify', 'give' and 'state' are similar command words.
- **Outline:** use sentences to give just the main points that are needed to make clear that you know and understand something.
- **Suggest reasons for:** this is similar to 'explain', except that there may not be an accepted correct answer. Marks are awarded for thinking out why something might be as it is and coming up with rational ideas.

■ Practise examination-type questions from the specimen paper and past papers published by your exam board, as well as those in the activities menu at the end of each chapter and in the *AS Travel and Tourism Student Workbook*.

■ Stick to the point with your answers to the questions. Refer back to the question wording to ensure you both satisfy its instruction and avoid irrelevance. Make use of appropriate case-study knowledge to illustrate your points.

■ Revise thoroughly.

Coursework advice

■ Remember your portfolios are assessments of what you know, understand and are able to do.

■ Learn and understand underpinning theoretical knowledge first. This includes learning and practising the application of your knowledge and understanding to case-study examples of real travel and tourism industry organisations or destinations first.

■ Make use of this book and the *AS Travel and Tourism Student Workbook* that accompanies it, as well as the activities menu at the end of each chapter.

■ You should have acquired the knowledge, understanding and skills needed for at least the first assessment task you are set before embarking upon it.

■ Develop, improve and practise the required skills, such as customer service skills, before they are assessed.

■ Complete one assessment task at a time to build your portfolios for Units 2 and 3.

■ Give proof of your research by quoting the sources you have used. Good practice is to identify each source within any text you produce and cross-reference it with a list of sources. For example, if you have used some

figures from the Statistics on Tourism and Research UK website (**www.staruk.org**), you should name the source next to the figures and quote it again in a references section at the end of your portfolio.

- Meet deadlines you have agreed or been set. Consider breaking down an assessment task into several parts and plan mini-deadlines for each.
- Follow carefully the wording for each assessment task and ensure you do exactly what it says. Make sure you understand what the wording requires at different levels of achievement.
- Aim high.
- Act on feedback to ensure success at your target level of achievement.

The travel and tourism industry

The travel and
tourism industry

Starter: defining travel and tourism

Travel and tourism is not only about holidays. It is about people going to visit somewhere else, and what they do while they are there. Tourism can be defined as 'voluntarily visiting a place other than that where one normally lives and works, for a short period of time with the intention of then returning home'.

Purposes of tourism

Visiting friends and relatives (VFR), **leisure** and **business tourism** are the three main types of tourism. Leisure tourism is when people go away to have fun, relax, sightsee, experience different cultures, visit attractions or take part in or watch sporting events. Business tourism is when people travel in connection with their work, e.g. to attend conferences and meetings.

People may also be called tourists when they move for a short period of time to another place for any other reason, such as for educational purposes or medical treatment.

The travel and tourism industry

Travel is the movement of people to reach their destination, the moving around they do while they are there and their return journey home. Travel can be:

- by air
- by sea, e.g. on cruise ships and ferries
- overland, e.g. by train, car or minibus

The travel and tourism industry is the increasingly interlinked set of organisations that provide for the travel and tourism needs of people. It includes organisations such as **travel agencies** and **tour operators,** as well as **transport providers** or **transport principals** such as airlines, coach and rail companies, and cruise-ship and ferry operators. Other travel and tourism organisations provide for the needs of tourists at their destination or at stops along the way. Examples include **accommodation providers** like hotels, **visitor attractions** and **tourism information providers** such as local tourist offices (Figure 1.1).

*Figure 1.1
The travel and tourism industry includes many types of organisation*

Types of tourism

Domestic tourism involves people taking trips or holidays in their own country. A New Yorker attending a business meeting in Chicago or visiting relatives in Florida would be a domestic tourist in the USA. If the New Yorker's family were to spend a holiday in southern France, they would be **incoming tourists** as far as France is concerned, while simultaneously being **outbound tourists** as they leave the USA.

The two countries most visited by outbound tourists from the UK in 2003 are neighbouring EU countries Spain and France. Of the top ten, only the USA is outside Europe.

Figure 1.2 gives information about inbound tourism to the UK.

Discussion point ⬤

Why is the USA so popular with UK outbound tourists? Over 3.6 million visited the USA in 2003.

Figure 1.2 Inbound tourists to the UK: visits and spending for the top ten countries, 2003

Source: Travel Trends 2003

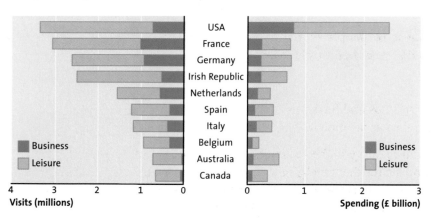

Support your learning

Information sources

1 Travel agents have brochures published by tour operators.

2 The UK government publishes travel and tourism statistics on the internet that you can access via the National Statistics website at **www.statistics.gov.uk**. Another valuable internet site for investigating UK travel and tourism is the Statistics on Tourism and Research UK website at **www.staruk.org**.

Skills builder

1 Analysing statistics means more than simply describing what the data tell you. It means breaking down the information into parts to examine it more closely, suggesting reasons for the figures you are studying before reaching a conclusion.

2 To evaluate means to give value or weight, balancing the strengths and weaknesses to come to a judgement.

Activities menu

1 a State four purposes of tourism other than leisure tourism.
  b Distinguish between domestic and inbound tourism.

2 Using a tour operator's brochure to help you, identify examples of:
  a three leisure tourism activities available to tourists on one named holiday
  b a range of travel and tourism organisations providing for the needs of customers

3 Research and analyse the number of visits made to the most popular foreign countries by UK tourists. The National Statistics website at **www.statistics.gov.uk** will help you. Find the data you need and break them down into EU and non-EU countries. Describe the information shown and suggest some reasons.

4 Use Figure 1.2 to evaluate the contribution made to inbound tourism to the UK by visitors from the USA in 2003.

The travel and tourism industry on the inside

Products and services

Products

The travel and tourism industry provides a wide range of products and services. Products are what travel and tourism organisations offer for sale. For example, travel agents offer for sale the package holidays featured in a tour operator's brochure. All these package holidays are products. An airline offering to sell a return flight from Manchester to Amsterdam is offering that product for sale.

The products of travel and tourism organisations are often:
■ intangible, which means they cannot be touched physically
■ perishable, which means they do not last
■ non-standardised, which means they do not perfectly repeat each other

For example, if travellers buy a one-way Eurostar train journey from London Waterloo International to Paris Gare du Nord, although they may be able to touch the train and their ticket, the product they have bought is the journey. This is intangible. Once they have arrived in Paris, the journey is over, so it is perishable. Although other travellers may make the same journey the following day, their experience may not be identical and it is in this sense that the product may be described as non-standardised.

Of course, there are exceptions. For example, if a hotel offers bed and breakfast accommodation, the breakfast is clearly perishable but it is also tangible, although the main product (the stay at the hotel) remains intangible.

Services

Services are the assistance travel and tourism organisations provide for their customers. In a tourist information office, staff may provide services such as telling customers about local attractions and booking accommodation for them. The provision of customer service is essential for travel and tourism organisations to sell their products. Topic 2 of this book and Unit 2 of the AS Travel and Tourism course cover travel and tourism organisations' customer service provision.

Seasonality

The delivery of travel and tourism services is often seasonal. Seaside resorts in the UK and the Mediterranean have definite **peak seasons** in mid-summer when the weather is warmer, sunnier and drier, and more people — including children in family groups — have their main annual holiday from work, school or college. The peak season is the busiest time of year when visitor and passenger numbers reach their annual maximum levels. The **high season** and **low season** are the busy and quiet periods of the year. In the Mediterranean, tourism still goes on in the low season — for example, the Spanish Costas are popular with elderly British tourists in the winter because, although it is not as warm and sunny at that time of year, such destinations have a Mediterranean climate with mild winters compared to the UK.

In the peak season tour operators and other travel and tourism organisations are able to charge higher, **premium** prices. Either side of the peak is the **shoulder season** when numbers of customers are still high but not maximal, and organisations may offer slightly lower prices to try to attract more customers. In September, for example, tour operators may offer lower-priced package holidays to destinations such as the Greek Islands.

Commercial and non-commercial organisations

Commercial organisations

The travel and tourism industry is dominated by commercial organisations such as travel agencies, tour operators, hotels and airlines. Commercial organisations are run to make money. There may be times when they make a loss, but the characteristic long-term aim of any commercial organisation is profit. Travel and tourism organisations in this category are said to belong to the private sector of the economy.

The **private sector** is one of the three sets of business areas that make up the UK economy. The others are the **public sector** and the **voluntary sector**, both of which are non-commercial organisations (see p. 9). In travel and tourism, the word 'sector' is also used to mean a key component of the travel and tourism industry. The sectors of the travel and tourism industry are:

- travel agents
- tour operators
- transport providers
- accommodation providers
- visitor attractions
- support services, such as tourist boards and tourist information and guiding

The six sectors of the travel and tourism industry are dealt with in detail in Chapter 1.4.

Private sector organisations are owned either by individuals (solely or in partnership) or by their shareholders. Shareholders are people who have bought a share of a company, which is run on their behalf by its directors and management. Shareholders expect a return on their investment, often in the form of an annual payment called a dividend. Profitable travel and tourism companies may pay bigger dividends.

Case study: Expedia

Expedia is an online travel agency. Customers can access its website at **www.expedia.co.uk** to book travel, accommodation and other tourism products and services. Table 1.1 (overleaf) summarises the products and services available via Expedia's UK home page.

Expedia's products

Among Expedia's products are some that are purely travel products (air flights, for example) and some that are purely tourism because they are for customers at a destination (or at some staging point along the way). Examples of the tourism branch of the travel and tourism industry are hotel stays and theme park admissions. **Independent travellers** commonly buy products that are purely travel or tourism. Such travellers are tourists who make their own arrangements to build into a trip they have created themselves. In other words, they book their travel and accommodation as separate items, possibly from different **online bookers** or directly from transport and accommodation providers such as airlines and hotels.

Other products in Expedia's range include elements of both travel and tourism. **Package holidays** and **tailor-made holidays** fall into this category. Package holidays comprise separate items that a tour operator

Industry branch	Products	Services
Travel	• Air flights • Car hire • Eurostar rail travel	• Online booking • Online information such as flight timetables
Tourism	• Airport transfers • Hotel accommodation • Ski and snowboard rental • Sightseeing tours • Admission to shows and events, including sporting events • Theme park admissions	• Online tourism guides to destinations • Online maps of destinations
Travel and tourism	• Package holidays • Tailor-made holidays • Insurance • Corporate travel (including accommodation)	• Online customer support • E-mail alerts of special offers • Personalised online accounts

Table 1.1 Expedia's products and services

Discussion point

Why does a commercial travel and tourism organisation such as Expedia provide online services free of charge?

has put together. A typical **mass tourism** package holiday advertised in a tour operator's brochure found in a high-street travel agent includes return air travel, transfers between the destination airport and accommodation in a hotel or self-catering apartment. Self-catering means customers cook their own meals or eat out. Mass tourism involves the commercial movement of large numbers of tourists, usually for leisure purposes like holidays. The development of mass tourism is described in Chapter 1.3.

Tailor-made holidays are customised packages. A customer is able to use an online facility, such as the Expedia website, to compile a self-assembly package by adding together separate travel and tourism elements. Tour operators such as Kuoni and Cox and Kings offer tailor-made holidays that customers may book directly with them or via a travel agent. **Direct selling** occurs where a tour operator and a customer deal with each other directly without using a travel agent as an intermediary.

Expedia's services

Services provided via the Expedia website include online booking of its products. In addition, information about its products is provided. This includes access to free tourist information about destinations and their attractions, with options to access and print online maps and driving directions. Other services include providing access to insurance

cover and setting up personal online accounts so that customers can review the progress of any arrangements they are making. Like many commercial organisations, Expedia offers a changing list of special deals that can be communicated to customers by e-mail.

Non-commercial organisations

Non-commercial travel and tourism organisations include the tourist boards that run tourist information centres in the UK. Figure 1.3 is a map of the ten English tourist board regions.

Non-commercial organisations belong to either the public or the voluntary sector of the economy. Public sector organisations are publicly owned. This means they are run using money collected from taxes paid by members of the public to the government and local councils. VisitBritain is the principal public sector organisation involved in promoting the UK as a tourist destination.

Figure 1.3 Tourist board regions in England

Case study: Tourism and the government in the UK

VisitBritain receives money from the government to market England and Britain to the rest of the world. In 2003–04, funding from the Department for Culture, Media and Sport (DCMS) totalled £35.5m for promoting Britain overseas as a tourist destination, and £14.1m for marketing tourism to England within the UK.

The DCMS champions the tourist, creative and leisure industries in the UK and is responsible for government's policy in all of them. This includes domestic tourism in England and incoming tourism to Britain. Scotland and Wales have devolved governments. Tourism policies for each of these are decided locally in cooperation with the DCMS. Since 2003, responsibility for tourism in the English regions has been devolved to the regional development agencies.

Sixty per cent of VisitBritain's staff are based overseas in Britain's key tourist markets, working to attract overseas tourists to Britain. The organisation's main website at **www.visitbritain.com** is a tool used for the same purpose, and a useful information source for travel and tourism students. The VisitEngland landing page on the internet is part of VisitBritain's marketing of England as a tourist destination.

The Wales Tourist Board (WTB) is the leading public sector agency for tourism in Wales. It encourages tourists to visit Wales and develops tourist amenities and facilities. Most of the WTB's funding comes directly from the National Assembly for Wales in Cardiff. Some additional money comes in as EU grants and from private sector organisations.

VisitScotland is the equivalent agency for Scotland. VisitScotland markets Scotland as a destination for leisure activities and domestic business tourism within the UK and overseas as an inbound destination. It works in collaboration with VisitBritain and employs about 200 people at its offices in Edinburgh and Inverness and at its visitor centre in London. The Scottish Executive, which is Scotland's devolved government, appoints VisitScotland's chairman.

The Northern Ireland Tourist Board (NITB) is responsible for developing tourism in Northern Ireland and promoting the province as a tourist destination. The NITB also advises the government's Department of Enterprise, Trade and Investment (DETI) on the development of tourism in Northern Ireland.

> **Discussion point**
>
> Given that the travel and tourism industry is largely composed of commercial organisations, why is taxpayers' money invested in organisations like VisitBritain?

Small- to medium-sized enterprises (SMEs)

Many businesses in the travel and tourism industry are small- to medium-sized enterprises (SMEs). Small firms are those with less than 50 employees and medium-sized ones are defined by the EU and the UK government as having at least 50 but less than 250 employees. Family-run hotels are examples of SMEs. Figure 1.4 shows such a hotel in the Lake District.

The roles of SMEs in travel and tourism are interrelated, so they often work closely together. For example, a hotel like the one in Figure 1.4 may not have the facilities to provide for all the leisure needs of its customers — it may not have a gym or a swimming pool. One solution is to come to an arrangement with a neighbouring larger hotel that has its own leisure club so that it will allow the smaller hotel's customers to use the club. By the same token, the larger hotel may wish to attract coach parties and can cooperate with a coach tour operator from outside the area that wants to sell customers mini-

Figure 1.4
The Skelwith Bridge Hotel, near Ambleside in Cumbria

Discussion point

Why would the management of a large hotel consider opening the doors of its leisure club to a smaller neighbouring rival?

breaks to the Lake District. Such coach-operating firms are travel and tourism organisations that are often small- to medium-sized enterprises (Figure 1.5).

Figure 1.5
Coach operators are often SMEs

Support your learning

Information sources

1 For information about incoming and domestic tourism facilities and attractions in the UK, try **www.visitbritain.com**.

2 For information about individual hotels, sources include visitor and tourist guides, promotional materials such as leaflets and the internet.

Skills builder

Use search engines on the internet, such as Google's UK pages, to seek useful websites. Knowing the actual web address often does not matter.

Activities menu

1 Begin to compile a glossary or dictionary of key travel and tourism terms using those in the Topic 1 Starter and in Section 1.1. Add new terms as you learn them. You might find it convenient to do this electronically.

2 Put together a chart summarising the key differences between commercial and non-commercial (public sector and voluntary) travel and tourism organisations. Include examples of each, featuring both SMEs and large travel and tourism organisations.

3 Research and analyse the range of products and services provided by a hotel similar to the one in Figure 1.4.

4 *Vocational scenario*

 Working as part of a consultancy team for a travel agent, your brief is to investigate the products and services provided by competing online agencies. Evaluate the range of products and services provided by one online booking agency other than Expedia.

The travel and tourism industry in the world

The travel and tourism industry operates in the real world. Organisations in the travel and tourism industry move people from one place to another. The world itself is constantly changing — physically, politically and economically — and these changes affect the travel and tourism industry. At the same time, the industry itself is undergoing constant change. As some organisations change, others are affected. Changes within the industry and in the world in which it operates create pressures on the travel and tourism industry.

Internal and external pressures

Internal pressures

Internal pressures arise within the industry and cause its organisations to change. For example, the rise of **budget airlines** has caused other airlines to consider reducing their fares. Budget airlines are air-transport providers that seek to offer customers cheaper air fares. They are sometimes referred to as **no-frills airlines** because one way of achieving lower fares is to cut some extra services that airlines have provided traditionally, such as free in-flight meals. Passengers may be able to buy food onboard the aircraft or take their own.

Budget airlines have brought the costs of air travel down by:
- using the internet to reduce booking costs
- **ticketless travel**, whereby passengers receive e-mailed e-tickets with their travel details and booking reference number when they book online
- maximising the use of aircraft so that they are in service as much as safely possible
- simple-service models that do away with luxuries like individually designated seats, through-tickets with other airlines and free catering onboard

- rapid airport turnaround times and reduced price **landing charges** agreements with the airports — landing charges are fees airlines pay airports for the right to land their planes
- using information and communication technology (ICT) for their administration

Examples of budget airlines operating in the UK include easyJet and Ryanair. These organisations have grown rapidly since the 1990s. Figure 1.6 is a map of easyJet routes from London Stansted in 2005.

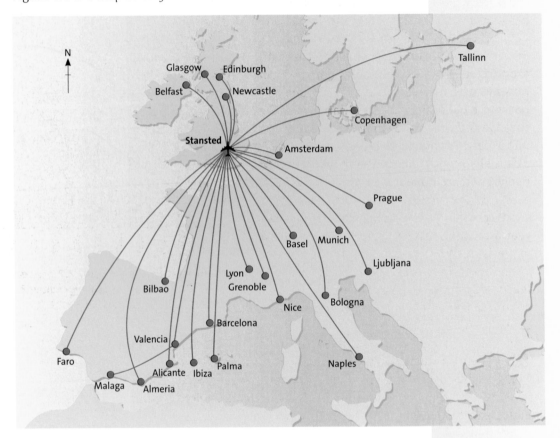

Flag-carrier airlines are national airlines. Like British Airways (BA), these organisations may belong to the private sector but they carry the name and flag of their country as well as some national prestige. Other flag-carrier airlines include Air France, KLM (the Dutch flag-carrier) and Air India. The rise of budget airlines has meant stiff competition for these companies and some have introduced cheaper fares in response.

Figure 1.6 easyJet routes from London Stansted, 2005

Case study: easyJet

The UK budget airline easyJet began operating in 1995. Figure 1.7 shows the growth in easyJet passenger numbers to 2004. In 2004, over 24 million passengers flew on easyJet flights, more than 800 times as many as in its first year of operation. The most rapid growth occurred in 2002–03, when passenger numbers nearly doubled and easyJet and Ryanair surpassed British Airways in the numbers of passengers flying with them. However, every year has shown an increase and figures for early 2005 showed 26% more passengers carried than during the same period the year before.

The particularly rapid growth in 2002–03 was fuelled by easyJet merging with another budget airline called Go, which had been established by British Airways as part of its strategy to compete with no-frills carriers. This year also saw easyJet expand its operation in Paris with new services to Barcelona, Marseilles, Milan, Nice and Toulouse, as well as the launch of new technology allowing passengers to view and change their bookings online for the first time. easyJet also set up a base in Berlin, adding 11 new routes to its network.

By comparison, 2003 saw a 5% decrease in the number of passengers travelling with British Airways and a 42% rise with Ryanair. Low-cost airline passenger numbers accounted for 68% of the total. The number of passengers flying on higher-priced charter flights also fell by 5%.

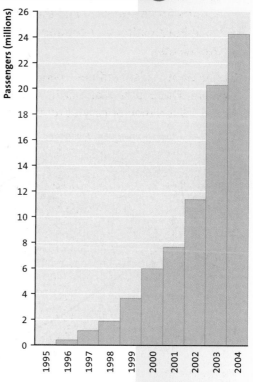

Figure 1.7 *easyJet passenger growth, 1995–2004*

External pressures

External pressures are those from outside the industry. Transport providers like airlines use a lot of fuel and can be placed under pressure from rising oil prices. In addition, major events such as natural disasters, disease outbreaks and terrorist activities affect where tourists want to go and how they can get there.

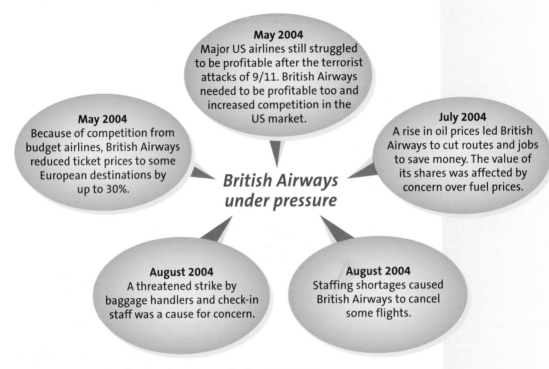

May 2004
Major US airlines still struggled to be profitable after the terrorist attacks of 9/11. British Airways needed to be profitable too and increased competition in the US market.

May 2004
Because of competition from budget airlines, British Airways reduced ticket prices to some European destinations by up to 30%.

July 2004
A rise in oil prices led British Airways to cut routes and jobs to save money. The value of its shares was affected by concern over fuel prices.

British Airways under pressure

August 2004
A threatened strike by baggage handlers and check-in staff was a cause for concern.

August 2004
Staffing shortages caused British Airways to cancel some flights.

***Figure 1.8** Internal and external pressures affecting BA, 2004*

Figure 1.8 shows some internal and external pressures affecting British Airways in 2004. The rising price of oil was an external pressure on the airline that year and led it to cut costs. The later pressure, a threatened strike in August, was internal, but possible redundancies and staff discontent cannot be totally separated. Internal and external pressures on travel and tourism organisations are often linked. Competition from budget airlines like easyJet and Ryanair is a pressure that is external to the organisation but internal to the travel and tourism industry. This is a second illustration of how, in practice, classifying pressures on travel and tourism organisations as internal or external is not always as straightforward as it may seem in theory.

Case study: The Indian Ocean tsunami

A tsunami is a huge wave of water created by an earthquake beneath the floor of the sea that can have devastating effects on coastal regions. Coasts are often regions of substantial tourism development.

On 26 December 2004, a powerful earthquake occurred beneath the Indian Ocean and the resultant tsunami created a disaster zone

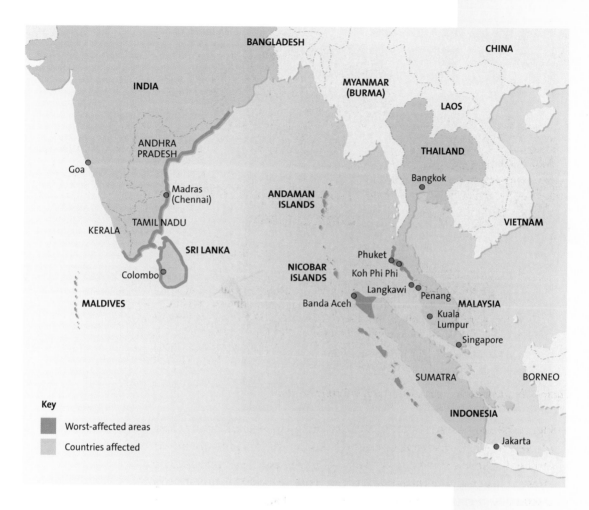

Figure 1.9 *Areas worst affected by the 2004 Indian Ocean tsunami*

around its shores from Africa to Indonesia. Many more than 200,000 people are believed to have lost their lives. Figure 1.9 is a map of the worst-affected areas. Figure 1.10 shows a hotel in the affected area after the tsunami hit.

In the aftermath of the disaster, tourism to the affected areas fell. Some resorts such as Khao Lak in Thailand were badly damaged and in 2005 were expected to take 3 years to rebuild and recover their tourist trade. However, in the Maldives, although widespread flooding caused 24 of the 87 resorts to remain closed 6 weeks later, the other 63 were open as normal but their **occupancy rates** (the percentage of hotel rooms occupied) were down by 40%.

Media coverage of the tsunami caused some tourists to stay away from the affected areas partly because of safety fears and partly out of sensitivity to the idea of holidaying in a disaster zone.

Figure 1.10
Hotel in
Phuket,
Thailand after
the tsunami

Topfoto

Discussion point ⬤

Were tourists who decided to stay away from the tsunami-affected areas (out of sensitivity to the suffering of local people) doing the right thing?

Impacts of travel and tourism

Travel and tourism also affect the world, both positively and negatively. Impacts may be classified as **economic**, **environmental** and **sociocultural**.

Economic impacts

Positive economic impacts

The economic impacts of travel and tourism are those connected with wealth and money. On the positive side, tourism creates jobs, and the local people employed in those jobs are paid wages that they spend in the local economy. Other local businesses, which may not be travel and tourism businesses, prosper as a result, feeding more money into the local economy and creating more jobs. This is called the **multiplier effect**. Local governments in parts of the less economically developed countries (LEDCs) of South and Central America, the Caribbean, Africa, the Indian Ocean, South and Southeast Asia and the islands of the Pacific Ocean are often keen to develop tourism for this reason. In more economically developed countries (MEDCs) like the UK, similar positive economic impacts are often the hope of **agents of tourism development** in areas of **economic regeneration**.

Agents of tourism development are individuals or organisations involved in developing tourism in a given place. They may include construction companies, private sector travel and tourism organisations, such as hotel owners, and public sector organisations, such as local councils, often working together in partnership. In the UK, formerly rundown inner-city areas — often in dockland and riverside locations — have been regenerated in recent years. Tourism development has been a major part of this process in cities throughout the UK such as Edinburgh, Manchester, London, Bristol, Newcastle and on Merseyside.

Negative economic impacts

In some cases, the jobs brought to a destination by travel and tourism organisations are **seasonal**. This is a problem traditionally experienced by seaside resorts in the UK such as Scarborough, where the winter unemployment rate rises. A second negative impact is **economic leakage**. This occurs where the wealth brought to a destination by travel and tourism leaks away to somewhere else. It is a problem that has been experienced by some LEDCs, for example where foreign-owned hotel chains have been established. Although the hotel company may pay taxes locally, its profit belongs to a large organisa-tion whose headquarters may be overseas (often in an MEDC in Western Europe, North America, Japan or Australasia). If **migrant workers** (employees whose permanent home is elsewhere in the country or abroad) are used, the problem can be worsened because they are likely to send some of the money that they earn home.

Environmental impacts

The very act of travelling can have negative environmental impacts. Aircraft, ships, trains, cars and coaches all consume fuel. Emissions from road transport and aircraft in particular can have damaging effects on the environment through atmospheric pollution. Pollution caused by noise and waste disposal can also be downsides of tourism if they are not managed properly. For example, tourist resorts in areas with coral reefs in the Maldives have experienced some damage as a result of water pollution from untreated waste water from hotel bathrooms.

Clearing land for building tourist facilities such as hotels changes the natural environment in ways that may be seen as detrimental. For example, natural vegetation and animal habitats may be lost and there may be impacts on the land's natural drainage system increasing the risk of flooding.

However, tourism can also bring environmental benefits. Landscaping often accompanies tourist developments such as hotels, seaside resorts and **purpose-built resorts** like the Disneyland complexes. This leads to artificial environmental change that may have a positive impact. In hot countries, coastal marshes may be breeding grounds for mosquitoes and a health risk for the transmission of diseases such as malaria. The drainage of such swamps adjacent to tourism developments can be beneficial to local inhabitants too and will probably be seen by them as an environmental improvement.

The tourist appeal of some destinations, for example National Parks and coral reefs, is based largely on the natural environment. These environments are often fragile and the impacts of tourism can be damaging. However, there is also a need to conserve the environment in order to ensure that tourists keep coming in the long term. **Sustainable tourism** is tourism that is managed in order to ensure that the future of an environment and its culture is not irreparably damaged. **Ecotourism** is tourism which is intended to contribute to the protection of the environment, often involving travel to areas of natural interest in developing countries (Figure 1.11).

Topfoto

Figure 1.11
Ecotourism is a sustainable form of tourism aimed at protecting the environment and local cultures

Sociocultural impacts

The sociocultural impacts of tourism are those where people's ways of life are affected. While on the one hand tourism brings people from different places and cultures into contact with each other — creating the opportunity for increased understanding between different social groups — conflicts and frictions can also sometimes result. In domestic tourism in the UK, for example, friction can arise in bars and clubs at seaside resorts between local customers and tourist visitors. Tourists from places with different cultural standards from those upheld by some local people in a tourist destination can cause offence, often unintentionally. For example, in some countries wearing beachwear in town centres and on sightseeing trips to religious sites may be viewed as inappropriate.

Sensitive management of such issues by travel and tourism organisations, and by tourists themselves, can usually avoid such friction arising. For example, visitors to the main mosque in the centre of Male, the capital of the Maldives, wear modest clothing before entering. Tour operators can reduce any risk of friction by providing customers with information when they arrive at their destination. This can be done in a **welcome meeting** convened by the tour operator's **resort representative**.

In **tourist-receiving areas** in less economically developed countries (LEDCs), visits to local markets or watching performances of traditional dances and rituals can be part of the tourist experience. While this may help keep such events and activities alive, there is also a risk of them becoming distorted. For example, dances intended for certain special occasions may be adapted or performed to fit in with the tourists' schedule. Such corruption of traditional culture is widely regarded as having a negative impact. Sustainable tourism seeks to allow local people to benefit economically from visits by tourists without damaging their traditional way of life.

Tourism can increase the range of social facilities available for local people's own leisure. Hotels intended primarily to cater for tourists at UK seaside resorts such as Scarborough, inland conference centres such as Harrogate, and National Park towns such as Ambleside in the Lake District provide restaurants, function rooms which can be used for wedding receptions, and sport and fitness clubs that local people can enjoy and which would not be there were it not for the tourist trade.

Case study: Tourism Concern

Tourism Concern is a voluntary organisation that aims to reduce negative impacts of tourism. It is a member organisation of the Travel Foundation, a charity set up to promote sustainable tourism that includes the UK government, travel and tourism organisations such as the tour operator Thomson and other charities like Tourism Concern.

One of the campaigns run by Tourism Concern has been to highlight the impact of the growth of **trekking** tourism on local people in the world's mountainous regions. Trekking is long-distance walking, spread over several days or more, in a challenging environment such as mountains.

Trekking in the world's mountainous regions is an increasingly popular form of adventure holiday. Local porters carry tourists' belongings and equipment in regions including the Himalayas, the Inca Trail in Peru and at Mount Kilimanjaro, Tanzania.

Himalayan people (Sherpas) are famous for accompanying big-name mountaineers on Everest expeditions. Nowadays, they also accompany tourists. Increased numbers of tourists have meant that many Nepalese porters today are farmers from lowland areas, who are often no more used to the high altitudes than the tourists.

These Nepalese porters suffer four times more accidents and illnesses than Western trekkers, according to Tourism Concern, who have worked with tour operators in the UK so that, by 2005, 41 out of 80 trek operators had policies to look after the welfare of their porters. Figure 1.12 shows trek porters in the Himalayas.

Discussion point

Why do some commercial tour operators take notice of pressure groups such as Tourism Concern? How can it be in their interests to promote sustainable tourism?

Figure 1.12 Trek porters in the Himalayas

©John Van Hasselt/Sygma/Corbis

Support your learning

Information sources

1 The Travel Foundation website at **www.the travelfoundation.org.uk** acts as a portal to research member organisations, including Tourism Concern.

2 Media reports in the press, on television and on the internet provide up-to-date information about major world events and their effects on travel and tourism, as well as including advertisements for low-fare airline flights.

Skills builder

Look back over recent events that have affected travel and tourism. Enter the issue (for example, the impact of budget airlines) into an internet search engine and visit the websites of national newspapers that have featured recent reports.

Activities menu

1 Investigate the prices offered by a range of airlines, including budget ones, for travelling from the UK to a destination airport of your choice.

2 *Vocational scenario*
Imagine you are a trainer in the travel and tourism industry. Explain to a newly recruited staff member why reading a newspaper and watching the news is important for his or her job role as a customer adviser for a direct-sell tour operator.

3 Research and analyse the effects on travel and tourism of a recent major world event.

4 Evaluate the impacts of travel and tourism on a tourist destination you know or have visited.

1.3

The development of travel and tourism

It is possible to find examples of travel and tourism far back in history. Business tourism was a part of ancient civilisations such as Ancient Egypt, as merchants and government officials moved between cities. The rich of Ancient Greece and the Roman Empire owned villas in the countryside and by the coast, where they stayed to escape the heat of cities in summer. Religious pilgrimages are also a kind of travel and tourism — pilgrims have been visiting holy cities such as Canterbury, Rome and Makkah since the Middle Ages. However, until 200 years ago the majority of the population of the UK lived in the countryside and it was rare for ordinary people to travel outside their local area.

Mass tourism

Mass tourism — the movement of people, as tourists on a large scale — emerged following the Industrial Revolution of the nineteenth century. Prior to that, tourism for leisure had been largely the preserve of wealthy people — the elite. During the eighteenth century, young British aristocrats undertook the 'Grand Tour', exploring the art and culture of the rest of Europe by visiting a succession of city destinations such as Vienna, Venice, Rome and Paris, sometimes over several months.

In the UK, the building of railways helped make it possible for ordinary people to travel to the seaside on excursions and for holidays. At this time, the motor car had not yet been invented and the roads were still largely unpaved. Overland transport was horse-driven and slow until the trains brought about a transport revolution. The simultaneous development of steamships made voyages overseas more practical and cruises began to be developed as luxury holidays for the rich. With respect to mass tourism, steamships opened up the possibility of travel to Ireland for example, either for pleasure, such as on Cook's Tours (see the case study on pp. 34–35), or to visit friends and relatives (VFR).

The Industrial Revolution led to a complete turn around of how and where people lived. The majority came to live in industrial cities, working in factories for wages, and those who could afford to began to spend surplus money on trips out of the polluted cities to the cleaner air of resorts, often on the coast. Seaside towns connected by railway to major industrial areas began to thrive. By the early years of the twentieth century, referred to as the Edwardian era after King Edward VII, considerable development of piers, promenades, hotels, cafés, theatres, parks and pleasure gardens had taken place. Figure 1.13 shows Scarborough in 1904. The large building with domes is the Grand Hotel, which opened in 1867 and catered for tourism demand generated by the coming of the railway.

Reflections of a Bygone Age

Figure 1.13 *Scarborough in 1904*

Seaside resorts

Figure 1.14 shows some of the UK's major seaside towns and the industrial regions they were linked to by rail. Some, like Scarborough and Brighton, had pre-Industrial Revolution pasts as resorts. Scarborough has a claim to be the world's first seaside resort, having been a spa town where visitors could 'take the waters' since the seventeenth century. Visiting the seaside for health reasons was a trend begun by the wealthy elite before the coming of the railways. The Royal Pavilion in Brighton (Figure 1.15) was extended from an earlier version into the Indian-style palace by the architect John Nash. He worked for the then Prince Regent, who became George IV in 1820. The prince had visited Brighton since the 1780s for the sea air and to attend the balls and parties held there. His example helped to popularise the idea of seaside resorts as more than just places to visit for health reasons.

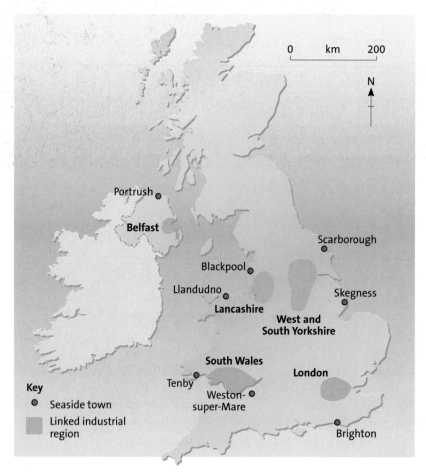

Figure 1.14 UK seaside resorts linked to industrial regions by rail

Topfoto

Figure 1.15 *The Royal Pavilion, Brighton*

In the interwar period (between the end of the First World War in 1918 and the start of the Second World War in 1939) Britain's seaside resorts continued to thrive despite economic difficulties such as the Great Depression of the 1930s, when there was large-scale unemployment. Holidaymakers from industrial areas went to stay for a week or a fortnight in accommodation ranging from small guest-houses or boarding houses to grand hotels that catered for the different levels of affluence in the target market of the urban population. Many continued to reach the resorts by rail, early motor cars being the preserve of a relatively small — though growing — number of wealthier people. Coach travel began. Initially, these mostly day-tripper buses were called charabancs (Figure 1.16) and were often open topped, but they provided cheap access to the coast for working people and their families.

Figure 1.16 A convoy of charabancs carrying employees of a Bolton firm to Blackpool, 1920

Topfoto

Holiday camps

The setting up of **holiday camps** in the 1930s and the introduction of the Holidays with Pay Act 1938 led to a boom in domestic tourism in the UK. Butlin's first holiday camp opened at Skegness in 1936. Holiday camps provided cheap accommodation in chalets for hundreds of people, with meals served in large dining halls and activities and amusements all included in the price of the holiday. Butlin's staff, employed to look after and entertain customers, wore characteristic red blazers and became known as 'Red Coats'. Holiday camps provided accommodation on an industrial scale and were able to keep down the unit costs of what amounted to an all-inclusive holiday because of the

economies of scale they could achieve, i.e. the cost savings that could be made by providing products and services on a large scale. Later in the twentieth century, economies of scale made by tour operators helped in the growth of the package holiday abroad.

Figure 1.17 shows the facilities at Butlin's holiday camp in Ayr, western Scotland in 1953.

The Holidays with Pay Act 1938 entitled employees to take time off work for holidays and still be paid by their employer. With the outbreak of war the following year, there was little time for this social reform to have much impact on the travel and tourism industry until the UK began to recover economically from the effects of the Second World War in the 1950s. For much of that decade, the seaside resort and the holiday camp continued to flourish.

Package holidays

The development of jet aircraft and the creation of package holidays led to more British people taking holidays abroad, especially around the Mediterranean Sea, from the 1960s onwards. Traditional seaside resorts began to decline.

Jet aircraft had been invented during the Second World War and were subsequently used commercially by airlines. The first commercial flights were made in 1952 but they were expensive and most passengers were wealthy or travelling for business. The development of the package holiday was the trigger that led to the changed direction from mass domestic tourism in UK seaside resorts to outbound tourism to the Mediterranean coasts, especially the Costas of Spain and its Balearic Islands of Mallorca, Menorca and Ibiza (Figure 1.18).

Four key factors had come together:
- **Socioeconomic change** including the prewar Holidays with Pay Act meant that most working people now had time and sufficient income to afford a 1- or 2-week holiday.

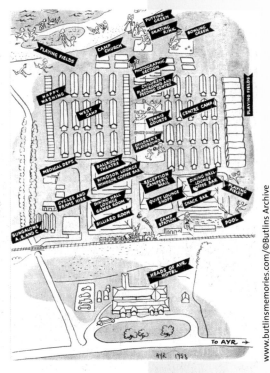

www.butlinsmemories.com/©Butlins Archive

Figure 1.17 The facilities at one Butlin's camp in 1953

Topfoto

Figure 1.18 Mass tourism in the Mediterranean: a crowded beach in Palma Nova, Mallorca

- **Technological innovations** in transport, including the development of jet airliners, made it possible to reach relatively far-away places, where the weather was warmer.
- **Product developments** of the package holiday and charter flights meant that complete holidays could be sold relatively cheaply because of economies of scale and without the need for travel knowledge on the part of the consumer.
- **Changes in consumer demand** as a newly affluent generation of tourists aspired to different goods and services, including holidays in places other than the UK seaside resorts of their childhood, where they could stay in modern hotels by the beach in sunny Mediterranean resorts.

High-street travel agencies increased in number as the retail outlets from which consumers could purchase package holidays advertised in the colour brochures of tour operators. Increasing computerisation of reservation systems made it possible for the travel consultant and customer to examine holiday availability and make instant bookings.

Meanwhile, increased car ownership led to the expansion of other holiday types, including motoring holidays — increasingly with caravans in tow — to continental Europe and especially France using car ferries to cross the English Channel. Tourism within the UK to countryside areas also grew, and in 1968 the Countryside Act established the Countryside Commission to administer National Parks in England and Wales. The following year, the Development of Tourism Act set up tourist boards to promote domestic and inbound tourism to the UK.

By the 1990s, several statistical milestones had been passed:
- more than 70% of British households owned a car
- over 30 million holidays abroad were taken by UK residents
- over a million trips a year were being booked by tourists using the internet

The twenty-first century

In the twenty-first century, holiday products are becoming more sophisticated. More people have travelled further and have more knowledge of destinations than in the past. They also have more money to spend on tourism. The travel and tourism industry has responded to these demand factors by expanding the range of destinations on offer, leading to increased supply. The growing global economy has led to increased business tourism not only in Europe but also to destinations including North America and the Middle and Far East. People are also much more able to visit friends and family in distant places. Growing numbers of expatriates working for international companies have fuelled this expansion in outbound tourism. The increasing multiculturalism of society has influenced inbound VFR tourism growth. Long-haul holidays to places like the Caribbean and the USA have become much more popular and there has been a growth in independent travel, assisted by the internet and tourists' increasingly wide travel experience and knowledge. Table 1.2 shows how the package holiday has started to decline.

Year	% of the UK holiday market on package holiday
1999	55
2000	55
2001	53
2002	52
2003	47

Table 1.2 The decline of the package holiday

Holidays catering for specific groups in the travel and tourism market have been a further development. Tour operators such as Saga (for the over 50s) and Club 18-30 cater for particular age groups. The hotel chain Couples, on the other hand, targets a specific customer group type. Such travel and tourism trends reflect the following social changes:
- An increasing number of retired people are in good health and have travel experience and money to spend. In the UK, the rising level of home ownership from the late twentieth century gave rise to the first generation of affluent older people en masse, as opposed to

just the wealthy elite. This expanding demand area has come to be known as the 'grey market' for travel and tourism organisations.

■ Younger adults with higher disposable incomes, and the social freedom to travel in groups apart from their families, have become another expanding sector of the market for travel and tourism. The rise in the average age at which women have their first child, more years spent in education, and higher wages and salaries among childless, younger adults (often in their 20s) are social trends that have been instrumental in the growth of travel and holidays deliberately targeted at this market segment, as well as the general growth of outbound tourism, including to long-haul destinations.

■ An increased proportion of DINKY (dual income, no kids yet) households and the increased popularity of, for example, 'weddings in paradise' packages are factors in the growth of couples-based holidays for the younger adult market, particularly to long-haul destinations.

Cruise holidays have enjoyed a revival. Until relatively recently, cruising was seen as a holiday for older tourists — often retired, sometimes travelling alone. For such customers, cruising offered a luxurious, safe and structured experience. Meals were formally served at least three times a day, and facilities, activities and entertainment were all laid on. Tour operators are now pitching cruises at families and younger adults in their 30s and 40s. Ocean Village, for example, is marketing such cruises in the Mediterranean and Caribbean seas under the slogan 'the cruise for people who don't do cruises' (Figure 1.19). Cruising in the waters of unusual parts of the world like Alaska and Antarctica have also come onto the market. This change has come about for the following reasons:

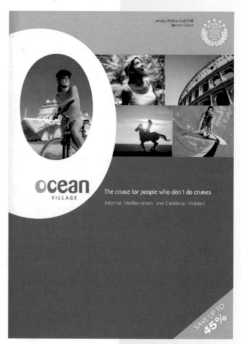

Figure 1.19 The Ocean Village brochure

■ As illustrated by the Ocean Village promotional material, marketing is targeting new market segments. However, promotion is only one element in the **marketing mix**. The marketing mix of 4Ps (promotion, product, price and place) is the combination of primary factors taken into account by a travel and tourism organisation when deciding how to market its products and services.

- Product change includes different activities both on board and onshore — more physical options, such as watersports, and less formal structuring to the typical day with meals being less restricted to set times and formal dress occasions such as balls reduced in number or abandoned. All these have been aimed at the younger potential customer and have created the 'new cruise'.
- The range of cruises on offer has been widened. Cruises around island groups, such as the Maldives and the Greek Islands, in smaller craft and to different destinations, including more river cruises such as along the Douro in Portugal, appeal to a wider market.
- The all-inclusive effect has also played a part. All-inclusive hotels have been a major feature of expanded long-haul tourism in the last 30 years. In many Caribbean destinations such as Jamaica and St Lucia, significant numbers of long-haul holidaymakers have rarely left their hotel during the holiday, finding plenty to occupy themselves on site and taking the occasional excursion. For such people, a 'new cruise' on a modern, well-equipped cruise liner provides the same benefits as the all-inclusive hotel while offering the additional advantage of organised excursions or activities at each port of call. Essentially, the 'new cruise' liner is a moving, all-inclusive hotel.
- Island hopping, e.g. in the Caribbean, refers to a style of holiday where tourists move from one island destination to the next. A cruise provides a relaxed way of doing the 'hopping' compared to, say, a series of short air flights with associated hotel transfers. Figure 1.20 shows a 'new cruise' route in the Caribbean.

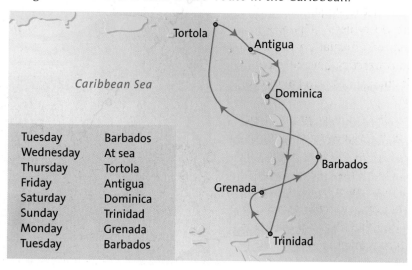

Caribbean Sea

Tuesday	Barbados
Wednesday	At sea
Thursday	Tortola
Friday	Antigua
Saturday	Dominica
Sunday	Trinidad
Monday	Grenada
Tuesday	Barbados

Tortola
Antigua
Dominica
Barbados
Grenada
Trinidad

Figure 1.20 A Caribbean 'new cruise' route

- Cruises appeal to the kind of customers who are conscious about the safety aspects of travelling alone. 'New cruises' appeal to such people who are below retirement age.

Discussion point

Which customer types may be attracted by 'new cruises'? Explain why.

Conclusions

Continuing innovation has led the travel and tourism industry to develop online booking agents such as Expedia (see Chapter 1.1) and budget airlines. 1995 saw the first flights by easyJet (see Chapter 1.2). Existing tour operators like Thomson have developed their own online options to complement their traditional travel agency marketplace. Travel agents have increasingly become national chains, developing new locations in hypermarkets and out-of-town shopping centres to attract customers who are less likely to shop in town centres. New types of travel agency, like the Trailfinders chain, cater for the more independent tourists who demand a flexible package customised to their needs. Increasing public awareness of environmental issues and concern about the impacts of tourism on destinations and their communities has led to increased sustainable tourism. Tour operators specialising in adventure holidays and ecotourism are among other recent developments.

Case study: Thomas Cook

Thomas Cook (Figure 1.21) was a Victorian tour operator. He organised a railway excursion from Leicester in 1841, charging customers a shilling (5p) for their return rail ticket and food for the journey. It was such a success that he set up in business running other railway trips to destinations including Scotland and London. In 1865, Cook's Tours were becoming well known and Cook was doing well enough to move his business to London, beginning to operate tours abroad and arranging trips that included travel to and accommodation in Egypt to see the pyramids. In 1872, Thomas Cook and Son was offering a 21-day round-the-world tour featuring a steamship crossing of the Atlantic Ocean, a stagecoach ride across North America, a Pacific crossing to Japan and an overland journey through China and India. The trip cost 200 guineas (£210) and would only have been affordable by very wealthy, as well as intrepid, Victorian tourists.

Figure 1.21
Thomas Cook

Mary Evans Picture Library

After Cook retired in 1879, his sons took over the family business. In the 1950s, at the dawn of mass tourism abroad, Thomas Cook and Son was, as a public sector travel agent, arguably the largest and most well-known travel agency in the world. However, its management misjudged the future when they decided not to enter the new package holiday market. Thomas Cook and Son did not take advantage of the new mass tourism trade and lost out to rival organisations.

Still suffering financial losses in 1972, the business was sold into the private sector. Thomas Cook AG is now owned by a German travel and tourism company and functions as a travel agent and tour operator with high-street outlets and online facilities via **www.thomascook.com**, as well as having its own charter airline, Thomas Cook Airlines.

Discussion point

How closely does the history of Thomas Cook and Son parallel the general development of travel and tourism since the Industrial Revolution?

Support your learning

Information sources

Public libraries stock local history books and may have archives of old photographs showing the development of local seaside towns.

Skills builder

1 Using a street map, plan and then carry out an exploration of a seaside town, annotating your map with evidence you find of the development of tourism in the resort.

2 Browse the catalogue of a library to compile a set of references about one period in the development of travel and tourism. Identify the main points of sources you find to produce a summary report.

Activities menu

1 Compile an annotated timeline to illustrate the main phases in the development of travel and tourism.

2 Explain the developments that have occurred in travel and tourism since the 1990s in terms of the four key factors that came together to cause the rapid growth of package holidays in the 1960s.

3 *Vocational scenario*
Imagine you are a member of staff in the tourist information office of a seaside town. You have been asked by your manager to produce a town trail leaflet that tourists can follow to trace the development of tourism in the town.
a Research the key events and locations you will need to produce your leaflet.
b Analyse the significance of these to the growth of tourism in the town.

4 Evaluate the extent to which your chosen seaside town has declined as a tourist destination since the 1960s. Comment on the success of measures designed to slow down this decline.

The structure of the travel and tourism industry

Commercial and non-commercial organisations

Commercial travel and tourism organisations are in business with the aim of making a profit (see Chapter 1.1). They belong to the private sector. Such organisations dominate the travel and tourism industry. Travel agents, tour operators, hotels and other accommodation providers are usually commercial organisations, as are many visitor attractions, although non-commercial organisations are more common in this sector.

Those travel and tourism organisations that are non-commercial belong to either the voluntary or the public sector. Voluntary organisations are often registered as charities. They aim to serve people by providing for a need without seeking to make a profit. Tourism Concern (see Chapter 1.2) is a voluntary sector charitable organisation that aims to reduce the negative impacts that tourism can have. The Youth Hostels Association (YHA) is an example of a voluntary sector accommodation provider.

Travel and tourism organisations belonging to the public sector (see Chapter 1.1) are managed on behalf of the public, funded by money from council and other national taxes that is distributed by the government via **quangos** (quasi non-governmental organisations) like VisitBritain. Quangos are not actually part of the government (so they are non-governmental), but they are accountable to it for how good a job they do (so they are not entirely non-governmental but quasi non-governmental).

The six sectors

Organisations in the travel and tourism industry belong to one of six sectors of the industry. As explained in Chapter 1.1, this is different from the three sectors of the economy (private, voluntary and public). The six sectors of the travel and tourism industry are:

- travel agents
- tour operators
- transport principals
- accommodation providers
- visitor attractions
- support services

A package holiday may include elements from all six sectors. Customers may book their holiday in a travel agency, choosing it from a brochure that was published by a tour operator. The tour operator has assembled the package from components including transport provided by, perhaps, a transport principal such as a charter airline and accommodation provided by a hotel company. While on holiday, the customer may experience a local visitor attraction such as a theme park and take advantage of a support service such as a crèche or kids' club. Figure 1.22 shows an example analysis of such a package holiday experience.

Figure 1.22 An example of a package holiday sector analysis

The holiday: *a 9-day coach tour of 'Scenic Brittany' booked by a recently retired married couple*

Travel agency
Thomas Cook, inside a Tesco hypermarket

The customers collected some brochures and returned the following day to book this holiday.

Tour operator
Shearings

The travel consultant books the 'Scenic Brittany' tour on behalf of the customers. The package is from Shearings's 2005 Europe and Worldwide brochure.

Transport principal
Shearings

Shearings operates its own fleet of coaches.

Accommodation
Provided by a local 3-star hotel, the Hostellerie Abbatiale in Le Tronchet.

(Hotels can receive star ratings from 1–5, according to the range of facilities they offer customers. A 3-star hotel is mid-range.)

The Hostellerie Abbatiale has 70 rooms, all en suite, with television and telephone. There is a restaurant and bar, and outside are extensive grounds and a tennis court.

Visitor attraction
An excursion to the chateau and lake at Combourg is included in the package.

Support services
Luggage handling is provided and, because the hotel has no lift, customers are able to request a ground-floor room if required.

Customers from older age groups appreciate someone to carry their luggage between the coach and their hotel room.

Vertical integration

Some organisations belong to just one sector of the travel and tourism industry. However, in today's industry, organisations often provide products and services across several sectors. In the case of a large organisation, this may be all six. The coming together of separate organisations to provide products and services for customers in different sectors of the industry is called vertical integration. Thomson-TUI is an example of a vertically integrated travel and tourism organisation (Figure 1.23).

Interdependency between sectors

Vertical integration is eased because of the close relationships that exist between the sectors. Indeed, provision in one sector may depend on that in another sector. For example, tour operators supply travel agents with brochures. To sell holidays from those brochures, the travel agent depends on the tour operator providing them. The link also holds true in the reverse direction. Although the tour operator can distribute brochures directly to clients, there is a high degree of dependency on the travel agent to stock them. The success of each as a business significantly depends on the sound management of the other.

Thomson Holidays is a division of TUI, an international group of tourism companies

Travel agents
Thomson (formerly Lunn Poly)
Travel House Group, including Callers Pegasus

Tour operators
Thomson
and specialist tour operators, including:
Magic Travel
Headwater Holidays
Villadeals

Transport principal
TUI airlines incorporating
Britannia Airways

Online and call-centre booking agents
Thomson Direct
Portland Direct
Team Lincoln
Manchester Flights

Figure 1.23 Thomson-TUI, a vertically integrated travel and tourism company

Travel agents

Travel agents sell travel and tourism products to the consumer. When mass tourism abroad began to develop in the 1960s (see Chapter 1.3), UK travel agents were typically small businesses, sometimes run by a single professional travel agent with a small clerical support staff, located in town centres to attract shoppers to come in to the agency to book a holiday or hotel, or to buy a travel ticket for a train, ferry or aeroplane journey. Many customers were leisure tourists, but others would be business tourists or those travelling to visit friends and relatives (VFR). Additional services like foreign currency were provided, as they still are.

As the travel and tourism industry developed, travel agencies experienced the following changes:

- **Ownership and size**: although some independent travel agencies remain as small businesses, many are now branches of chains. Some

Figure 1.24 Inside a travel agency — a travel consultant advising customers

— like Thomson, Going Places and Thomas Cook — are national organisations. In this respect, travel agencies have been affected in the same way as other high-street retailers.

- **Location**: as shopping habits have changed and the consumers of travel agency products and services have become car users, travel agencies have developed in new locations such as in hypermarkets and out-of-town shopping centres, while often retaining their town-centre branches.
- **Integration**: as the travel and tourism industry has become more vertically integrated, travel agents have become partners in large organisations with other providers (see Figure 1.23 for the example of Thomson-TUI).
- **Computerisation**: as computerised reservation systems became more sophisticated, travel consultants (people who work in travel agencies advising customers) have been able to confirm availabilities and prices for clients for a range of travel and holiday options as the customers sit with them. Travel agents have found it easier to customise holidays for clients using the internet. Firms like Trailfinders have consequently been able to discuss various component options with customers to assemble one-off packages for them. As with other retailers, increasingly sophisticated point-of-sale technology has enabled instant financial transactions like credit and debit card payments to be made.

The future of travel agencies

The growth of internet online booking has commonly been seen as a threat to the future of travel agencies on the high street. By 2003, fewer than half of the holidays abroad enjoyed by British outbound tourists were package holidays. Such holidays are not the sole product provided by retail travel agents, but they are essential to their survival. Increased access to the internet, greater customer experience of travel (breeding consumer confidence to make independent travel arrangements) and the attraction of the low fares offered by budget airlines are factors in the increasing threat travel agencies face. However, the market for traditional travel agency services, especially among less confident customers, such as elderly holidaymakers, remains large enough to ensure the continued presence of travel agencies on British high streets.

ABTA

The Association of British Travel Agents (ABTA) is the trade body to which UK travel agents belong. In the early days of mass tourism, there were a number of well-publicised bank-ruptcies, such as the collapse of the tour operator Clarksons, that left tourists stranded abroad. ABTA protects consumers against their holiday being spoiled if their travel agent (or tour operator) runs into financial difficulties while they are abroad. Customers can finish their holiday or, if they have not yet left home, have their money refunded so they can arrange an alternative.

As far as the travel and tourism industry is concerned, ABTA provides customer confidence and protects the **turnover** of member travel agents by means of insurance. Turnover is the total income of a business such as a travel agency or tour operator. ABTA's formation was an important milestone in the development of mass tourism abroad. Customers normally pay the full amount of their holiday well before they travel, so they need to feel confident that their money and their holiday will be safe, otherwise travel and tourism organisations would lose trade and money. As Figure 1.22 shows, organisations in all sectors of the industry could be affected by any loss of consumer confidence.

Tour operators

A tour operator puts together more than one component of a tourism trip. The package holiday made up of the components of airport transfer, flight and destination accommodation is a standard tour operator product. However, not all tour operations are concerned with such products. Tour operators exist for domestic, inbound and outbound tourism.

Domestic coach operators like Shearings and Wallace-Arnold organise coach holidays within the UK and on the continent. In addition, they provide for the touring needs of inbound tourists. While many inbound tourists from Europe travel with a coach operator from their homeland, others from within Europe and beyond come to the UK by other means — mainly by air. Such parties of tourists may want to travel beyond London, which the majority visit, to other destinations such as Shakespeare's birthplace Stratford-upon-Avon. A typical coach tour to a destination such as the Lake District or the Black Forest in Germany includes components of coach travel, catering, accommodation and excursions.

Tour operator businesses vary in size. Many travel and tourism organisations are small- to medium-sized enterprises (SMEs) (see Chapter 1.1). Smaller, independent tour operators may arrange tours and holidays within a **niche** or small **specialist market** such as skiing, or self-catering cottages and apartments in a certain locality. Many of these independent tour operators advertise in the classified advertisement sections of newspaper and magazine travel sections.

AITO

The Association of Independent Tour Operators (AITO) is a trade organisation that independent tour operators in the UK can join. Members display the AITO logo on their brochures to inspire confidence in new and potential customers. In 2005, AITO had 156 tour operator members. Members are independent companies, most of them owner-managed, specialising in particular destinations or types of holiday. They are carefully checked by AITO and are **bonded**. This means there is money for insurers to pay for the holidays of any tourists whose tour operator becomes bankrupt while they are on holiday. This is similar to the ABTA scheme. AITO also has a code of practice that includes clear and accurate descriptions of holidays in brochures and using customer questionnaires to monitor standards. AITO members are encouraged to raise awareness of **responsible tourism**, i.e. tourism that has the minimum negative impact on a destination and its people.

Transport principals

Organisations that provide transport for tourists are transport principals. They may be airlines such as British Airways and easyJet, ferry and cruise operators such as P&O, train companies such as GNER and Virgin Trains, coach firms such as Wallace-Arnold or car hire companies such as Avis, but any organisation providing any form of transport for a tourist to or from a destination or in and around a destination is a transport provider.

easyJet

Figure 1.25
Transport principals are organisations that provide a form of transport for a tourist

Scheduled and charter flights

Airlines may provide scheduled flights or charter flights, in some cases both. A scheduled flight runs regularly, according to a timetable or schedule, between named airports. Any member of the public can buy a ticket for a scheduled flight either directly from the airline — as is increasingly the case owing to the expansion of the internet — or through a travel agent.

Charter flights operate as a result of a special contract or charter. Tour operators may charter an aircraft to carry their passengers to a destination airport. By doing this, the tour operator can achieve economies of scale incorporating the flight in a holiday package for less than the total price of travel and accommodation added together. It is this sort of arrangement that enabled the boom in mass-market package holidays from the 1960s. Budget airline low fares, however, have cut the price of scheduled air travel so that charter arrangements are no longer necessarily cheaper. Charter flights may still run regularly — at the same time of the same day of the week during the holiday season — but tickets are not normally on general sale. Spare tickets may sometimes be sold off at a discount price.

Accommodation providers

Tourist accommodation may be **serviced** or **unserviced**. The key difference is the service of housekeeping.

Serviced accommodation

A hotel is a form of serviced accommodation. Guests' rooms are serviced regularly — beds are made, the room is cleaned and tidied, rubbish is cleared, any tea, coffee or minibar facilities are replenished and towels are changed. Other services may also be provided, such as meals, but they are not defining characteristics of serviced accommodation. A hotel offering room-only board arrangements is still providing serviced accommodation.

Figure 1.26 *Hotels are a form of serviced accommodation*

Table 1.3 summarises hotel board arrangements. In city destinations prices may vary between weekdays and weekends, with the latter being the cheaper. The hotel's target market during the week is likely to be business tourists whose companies are prepared to pay premium (high) prices to ensure their high-ranking staff are well rested and able to do the firm's business successfully on the day following an overnight hotel stay. As such demand does not exist at the weekend, hotel companies often offer discounted rooms to leisure tourists.

Type	Meaning
Room only	• Guests are provided with serviced accommodation in a room. The room may be en suite if it has a private bath or shower room attached. • The hotel may have a restaurant and/or offer room service, but these are optional extras and not part of the basic deal offered to the client. • Larger hotels may have minibars in guest rooms. These are small fridges containing soft and alcoholic drinks, and sometimes snacks such as nuts and chocolates. Guests are usually charged extra for items they consume from the minibar. • Many hotels offer guests in-room tea- and coffee-making facilities that are included in the room-only price.
Bed and breakfast	• Breakfast, usually in the hotel restaurant, is included in the price paid by the customer. • Sometimes breakfast in the room will be offered as an additional room-service option, for which the guest will usually be charged extra. • Room service is the delivery of food or drinks to the guests' rooms by hotel staff. Normally the guests order from a menu in their room by telephoning an internal hotel extension number.
Half board (UK) Demi-pension (Europe)	• An additional meal is provided in the deal offered to the guest. This is normally an evening meal served in the hotel restaurant.
Full board (UK) Pension (Europe)	• In addition to breakfast and evening meal, guests can have lunch in the hotel as an integral part of the price paid. • Hotels may offer to replace the restaurant lunch with a packed lunch for guests going on an excursion for the day. It would be rare, however, for the hotel's management to delete the cost of a meal not taken from a customer's bill.
All-inclusive	• Strictly speaking, this is still full board. However, in an all-inclusive hotel or resort, more of the customer's holiday needs are included in the price charged. • Drinks at the bar, leisure and sport facilities and use of the kids' club are typical extra inclusions. • Sometimes there may still be an extra charge for particularly costly items and services.

Table 1.3 Hotel board arrangements

Other forms of serviced accommodation include guesthouses, inns, motels, ship cabins and serviced apartments. This last type is a growing type of city accommodation appealing to the business market.

Unserviced accommodation

No catering or cleaning services are provided in unserviced accommodation. Tourists staying in apartments, cottages, canal boats, caravans, mobile homes and tents normally make their own beds. In some self-catering accommodation such as French **gîtes** (self-catering cottages and apartments in the countryside), customers may also be expected to clean the property at the end of their stay.

Visitor attractions

Tourists staying in a resort may be attracted to visit a natural feature such as a waterfall, a leisure facility such as a theme park, a historical site such as a castle, a cultural facility such as a museum or a sporting venue such as a football stadium. These are examples of visitor attractions. There is clearly a wide range. Some are natural attractions and others are built; some charge for admission and others either are free or ask visitors for a voluntary donation.

Durham City is a historic town in northeast England that attracts both domestic and inbound tourists. Many of them visit the cathedral, which is a **World Heritage site**. UNESCO (the United Nations Education, Scientific and Cultural Organization) specifically lists World Heritage sites because they are of great importance scenically, historically or culturally and deserve the attention of the world in their conservation. They are judged to be significant to the heritage of all the world's people. Admission to Durham Cathedral is free, but there is active encouragement to visitors to leave a financial donation to help in the upkeep of the building.

Visitor attractions may be operated by commercial or non-commercial organisations (both public sector and voluntary).

Support services

One key tourism support service is information provision. In the UK, tourism authorities including VisitBritain and VisitScotland, the Wales and Northern Ireland Tourist Boards and regional authorities, such as Visit London and the Northumbria Tourist Board, provide tourist information to the travel and tourism industry and to domestic and inbound tourists. Increasingly, this is done via the internet. The VisitBritain website at **www.visitbritain.com**, for example, is available in several languages to cater for the information needs of inbound tourists from around the world.

Tourist information offices in most UK towns serve the needs of leisure and business tourists by providing information and offering other support services such as hotel bookings. Other bodies such as the National Park authorities operate information services via visitor centres like Brockhole in the Lake District National Park.

Some support services are extras made available by a provider from one of the other five sectors of the travel and tourism industry. For example, staff at the concierge desk of a large hotel will give customers directions to an attraction, advise them about opening times and events as well as making bookings on their behalf. A tour operator's resort representative may run a children's club for clients.

The informal sector

In less economically developed countries (LEDCs), in particular, a significant number of people make a living through the economy's informal sector. The informal sector is that part of a country's economy that consists of the activities of people working independently of any employer or state bureaucracy. People working in the informal sector often work for themselves or for others without a formal contract of employment. They will commonly not be registered by the government for tax or regulatory purposes.

Figure 1.27 *A beach vendor selling goods to tourists*

©Mike McQueen/Corbis

In the travel and tourism industry, the informal sector offers a range of products and services to tourists, examples being beach vendors selling goods such as T-shirts, souvenirs, snacks and drinks and unofficial guides. In Caribbean destinations, hair braiding is popular too.

The informal sector is valuable to the economies of LEDCs as tourist money finds its way directly into the hands of local people. This sector can therefore be seen as helping to build the sustainability of tourism in a destination, since the guides and vendors are finding paid work and will spend their income in the local economy. One negative impact of tourism (see Chapter 1.2) is economic leakage when money brought into a destination by tourists leaks away again, for example as with the profits of a foreign-based hotel chain. The informal sector at least does not lead to economic leakage. However, there is no security of employment for such people and often little in the way of health and safety protection. If they do not pay tax, social developments in poorer areas, such as improved medical facilities, will not receive funding from tourism revenue.

The informal sector of the travel and tourism industry is not confined to LEDCs. People offering beach massage and touting for trade outside bars and clubs are commonplace in Mediterranean resorts. Trinket-sellers and street performers are also found at major tourist **honeypot sites** in Europe and North America. Honeypot sites are attractions that bring tourists together in a restricted locality in great numbers — like 'bees round a honeypot'. Places such as Battery Park, New York City (where boats for the Statue of Liberty start), Covent Garden in London and the Eiffel Tower in Paris come into this category.

Support your learning

Information sources

Classified advertisements in newspaper and magazine travel sections are valuable starting points for investigating independent tour operators. Many give website addresses that will enable you to carry out further research more quickly than sending for brochures.

Skills builder

Select from the breadth of information at your disposal when you carry out research. Organise a topic into categories and decide on how many examples you need (which may be only one) for each category. For example, for Activity 3 below, classify visitor attractions as commercial or non-commercial, natural or built and then target one attraction example from each category.

Activities menu

1 Identify organisations that belong to each of the six sectors of the travel and tourism industry. Classify them according to whether they are commercial or non-commercial organisations and note examples of relationships between them.

2 Select a holiday from a tour operator's brochure. Explain the contribution of the different sectors of the travel and tourism industry to the itinerary.

3 *Vocational scenario*
Imagine you work as a resort representative for a tour operator. You have been posted to a destination new to the company. Before you leave, your manager has asked you to compile a portfolio of visitor attractions for inclusion in welcome meetings.
a Research a range of visitor attractions available at the destination.
b Analyse the appeal of the attractions to three different customer types.

4 *Vocational scenario*
Imagine you are a travel journalist. You have been assigned by your editor to write an article evaluating support services offered to guests at a hotel belonging to an international chain. Space is limited and you have been given a maximum of 250 words, so you need to select your information carefully.

Investigating travel and tourism in a UK destination

Practical scenario

The travel and tourism industry in any UK destination can be investigated in terms of its:

- **structure**: the size and range of commercial and non-commercial organisations belonging to the six sectors of the industry and the links between them
- **products and services**: the range of products and services that the industry in the destination provides
- **internal and external pressures**
- **impact** on the destination and its people
- **development through time**: how the industry in the destination came to be as it is now

This chapter is a practical scenario intended to show you how to investigate the delivery of travel and tourism in a UK destination. Travel and tourism is an applied subject, so the principle behind this chapter is that you apply the content of Chapters 1.1 to 1.4 to a real UK destination yourself. A-level Travel and Tourism also has a vocational emphasis on developing practical skills that build your knowledge and understanding of an industry — the travel and tourism industry. Skills of research, communication, analysis, evaluation — as well as the skills of dealing with people, solving problems and working in a team — are all included. This chapter will point the way for you to apply your skills, knowledge and understanding to the investigation of the travel and tourism industry in a tourism destination in the UK.

To illustrate the approaches put forward, the example destination of Stratford-upon-Avon (Figure 1.28) is used.

Case study: Stratford-upon-Avon

Stratford-upon-Avon is a popular tourist destination. Figure 1.29 shows the location of Stratford in the UK. It is a market town dating back to medieval times, famous as the birthplace of the Elizabethan playwright William Shakespeare. Hundreds of thousands of tourists visit the town each year to see the historic properties associated with Shakespeare, go to the theatre and to enjoy the many attractions in the town and surrounding area. In 2004–05, about 400,000 people visited the tourist information centre in the town.

South Warwickshire Tourism markets Stratford-upon-Avon as a tourist destination that is part of 'Shakespeare Country'. Shakespeare Country also includes the towns of Warwick, Leamington Spa, Kenilworth and the countryside between them. One of the marketing techniques South Warwickshire Tourism has used on its Shakespeare Country website (**www.shakespeare-country.co.uk**) is to publish a

Figure 1.28 *Stratford-upon-Avon*

Courtesy of South Warwickshire Tourism

Figure 1.29 *The location of Stratford-upon-Avon*

map of leisure drives (Figure 1.30) to encourage tourists to explore the countryside beyond busy honeypot sites like Stratford itself. This relieves pressure on the travel and tourism industry in its town centre and spreads the positive — especially economic — impacts around south Warwickshire.

South Warwickshire Tourism is the local tourist board for Stratford-upon-Avon and Shakespeare Country and as such is a non-commercial public sector travel and tourism organisation. Providing tourist information is a support service, so that is the sector of the travel and tourism industry to which South Warwickshire Tourism belongs. Table 1.4 gives examples of Stratford-upon-Avon travel and tourism organisations belonging to different sectors of the industry and classifies them by size and type of enterprise.

The regional tourist board for Stratford-upon-Avon is Visit Heart of England. Nationally, it is marketed by VisitEngland, part of VisitBritain.

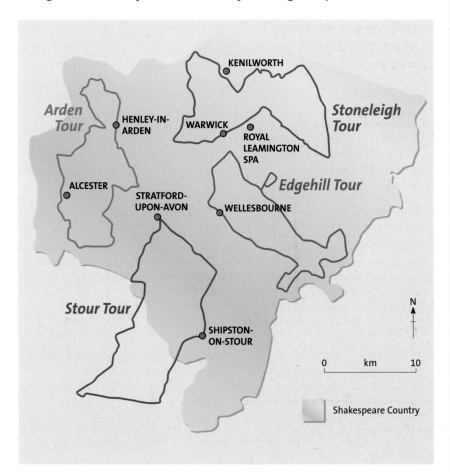

Figure 1.30
Leisure drives in 'Shakespeare Country'

Sector	Example organisation	Size and type of organisation
Travel agents	*Going Places Leisure Travel Ltd* Travel agents located in a UK destination provide products and services for travel away from the destination — aimed at local inhabitants rather than visitors. Travel agents elsewhere arrange for travel to the destination.	Large commercial organisation — a national chain with a Stratford-upon-Avon branch.
Tour operators	*RSC Theatre Tours* Arranges behind-the-scenes tours of the Royal Shakespeare Theatre (Figure 1.31). The theatre is a major visitor attraction in Stratford-upon-Avon.	The Royal Shakespeare Company (RSC) is a large, national, non-commercial organisation funded by public subsidy as well as by ticket sales and business sponsorship. RSC Theatre Tours in Stratford is a small part of that much larger whole.
Transport providers	*Shakespeare Tours* Shakespeare Tours provides a limousine airport transfer service to link Stratford to the London airports and Birmingham International Airport, among others. The company also acts as a tour operator by providing customised motor tours of Stratford and the nearby Cotswolds.	Commercial organisation; SME.
Accommodation providers	*Riverside Caravan and Camping Park* This campsite is one of the numerous accommodation providers. About 1.5 km from Stratford's town centre, it no longer accommodates tents but welcomes touring and motor caravans. Accommodation types in Stratford are varied and include hotels, guesthouses, bed and breakfast establishments, inns, camping and caravan sites and hostels.	A local, commercial travel and tourism organisation; SME.
Visitor attractions	*Anne Hathaway's Cottage* Managed by the Shakespeare Birthplace Trust, which owns five houses in and around Stratford that are connected with William Shakespeare, this world-famous thatched cottage was the childhood home of his wife, Anne (Figure 1.32).	The cottage can be categorised as an SME as it is part of the Shakespeare Birthplace Trust, a larger, non-commercial organisation.
Support services	*South Warwickshire Tourism* This local tourist board is an information provider that also acts as a travel agent and tour operator. For example, it sells themed tours of Stratford via its website (**www.shakespeare-country.co.uk**).	Tourist boards are non-commercial public sector organisations.

Table 1.4 Travel and tourism organisations in Stratford-upon-Avon

Figure 1.31 The Royal Shakespeare Theatre, Stratford

Courtesy of South Warwickshire Tourism

Courtesy of South Warwickshire Tourism

Figure 1.32 Anne Hathaway's Cottage

Research methods

To investigate the delivery of travel and tourism in a UK destination such as Stratford-upon-Avon, **primary** and **secondary research methods** can be followed.

Primary research methods

These are methods of research that lead to the collection of original data. They include:

- **Observation and survey**: going and seeing for yourself.
- **Questionnaires and interviews**: asking other people.

Secondary research methods

In this case you are collecting data that have already been collected and presented by someone else. A variety of types of source exist:

- internet websites
- books and periodicals, including travel guidebooks and the travel press
- tourism promotional materials, such as brochures and leaflets
- maps and photographs

Table 1.5 suggests the methods that can be applied to investigating the delivery of travel and tourism in a UK destination such as Stratford-upon-Avon, and Figures 1.33–1.35 are possible data collecting sheets you can adapt for use in your destination. People can be sensitive about their age, so you could complete tick lists at the ends of the questionnaires (Figures 1.34 and 1.35) after you have finished interviewing the person, but do it straight away so you don't forget. This introduces subjectivity. **Subjective views** are those for which personal judgement is necessary, as opposed to **objective views** which are formed without being influenced by personal opinion or bias. In this case, the degree of subjectivity, i.e. guessing someone's age, is sufficiently slight as to have little impact on your results.

Research aim	Research objective	Primary research techniques	Secondary research techniques
The structure of the travel and tourism industry in Stratford-upon-Avon.	The size and range of commercial and non-commercial organisations belonging to the six sectors of the industry and the links between them.	• Visit the destination. • Survey the organisations present. Record your results on a data collection sheet (Figure 1.33) and later on a blank street map of the town using colour coding (a different colour for each sector). Work as a team by sharing data between groups and pooling the results later.	• Use the internet. Local tourist board websites are useful starting points and often have links to extend your research. Start by entering your destination name in a search engine like Google (**www.google.co.uk**) and sample sites first to identify the most useful. • The *Yellow Pages* is a useful directory for identifying relevant organisations, which can be visited or researched further. If they have websites, you can use a search engine to find them — **www.yell.co.uk** is the *Yellow Pages* website. • Travel guidebooks such as the *Rough Guide to Britain* are useful sources for transport and accommodation providers and visitor attractions. • Tourism publicity materials can be obtained from the tourist information office.

Research aim	Research objective	Primary research techniques	Secondary research techniques
Products and services	The range of travel and tourism products and services that the travel and tourism industry in the destination provides.	• Visit the destination. • Survey the products and services provided by travel and tourism organisations by visiting them and making a record (Figure 1.33). • View displays and collect publicity information from the tourist information office. Pre-arrange an interview with a member of staff or, if there is a large enough group, a talk.	• Use the internet. Many individual travel and tourism organisations have their own websites that can be searched for. • Tourism publicity materials produced by individual organisations are useful. • Review media articles about the destination in the local and national press.
Pressures	The internal and external pressures on the industry.	• Survey numbers of visitors by doing a footfall count, for example at the tourist information office and major attractions. Work as a team by sharing data between groups and pooling the results later. • Observe and collect evidence of environmental, economic and sociocultural impacts by taking photographs and making annotated sketches or by marking impact sites on a base map. Look for positive as well as negative impacts. • Question visitors about the quality of their experience. Figure 1.34 is a sample visitor questionnaire. • Question local stakeholders about their attitudes. Figure 1.35 is a sample question-naire you can adapt for this. Stakeholders are people with an interest in an issue. Local stakeholders would include residents, business managers and the local council. • Interview expert witnesses such as travel and tourism professionals in the destination. Pre-arrange this and consider an e-mail interview for busy people.	• Use the internet as a source of useful statistical information. Sites worth researching include: **www.staruk.org** and **www.tourismtrade.org.uk**. • Review printed sources such as media articles about the destination in the local or national press. Media websites can be useful starting points.

Research aim	Research objective	Primary research techniques	Secondary research techniques
Development through time	How the travel and tourism industry in the destination came to be as it is now.	• Survey the history of the organisations by visiting them and making a record of your findings (Figure 1.33). • Question visitors about their past experiences in the destination. Figure 1.34 is a sample visitor questionnaire. • Question local residents and travel and tourism professionals about the past of travel and tourism in the destination. Figure 1.35 is a sample questionnaire for this. • Interview expert witnesses.	• Study local histories and old photograph/postcard collections. Public libraries are useful sources of this type of evidence, as is the internet.

Table 1.5 *Research methods for investigating travel and tourism delivery in a UK destination such as Stratford-upon-Avon*

Travel and tourism organisation

Name: _____

Address: _____

_____

_____

_____

_____

Nature

Ring as appropriate:

Commercial

Non-commercial

Size

Ring as appropriate:

Small
(<50 employees)

Medium
(50–250 employees)

Large
(>250 employees)

Products

_____

_____

_____

_____

_____

_____

_____

Services

_____

_____

_____

_____

_____

_____

_____

Figure 1.33 *Data collection sheet*

Figure 1.34 *Visitor questionnaire*

1 Where have you travelled from today?

☐ Local (from destination)

_____

☐ Tourist (from destination)

_____

If local, please use local/stakeholder questionnaire (Figure 1.35)

2 Which travel and tourism facilities have you used, or do you intend to use, during your trip?

_____

_____

_____

_____

3 Have you visited Stratford before?

☐ Yes   ☐ No

If yes, when? _____

What changes have you noticed in tourist facilities and numbers?

_____

_____

_____

_____

4 What impacts of tourism have you noticed on this visit?

_____

_____

_____

_____

Thank you

Age group of visitor (please tick one)

<16 ☐   17–25 ☐   26–35 ☐   36–49 ☐   50–65 ☐   66+ ☐

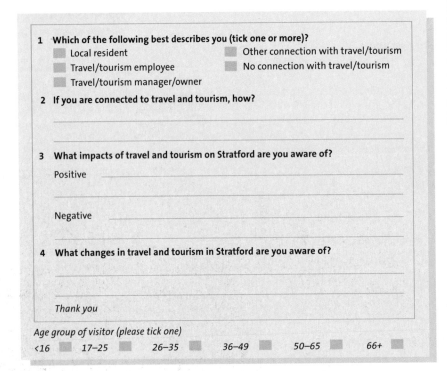

Figure 1.35 Local people/stakeholder questionnaire

1 **Which of the following best describes you (tick one or more)?**
Local resident
Other connection with travel/tourism
Travel/tourism employee
No connection with travel/tourism
Travel/tourism manager/owner

2 **If you are connected to travel and tourism, how?**

3 **What impacts of travel and tourism on Stratford are you aware of?**
Positive

Negative

4 **What changes in travel and tourism in Stratford are you aware of?**

Thank you

Age group of visitor (please tick one)
<16   17–25   26–35   36–49   50–65   66+

Discussion point
What are the strengths and weaknesses of the data collection sheet and questionnaires? How can they be adapted for your own research?

Support your learning

Information sources

Table 1.5 suggests relevant information sources.

Skills builder

Improve your skills in dealing with people by using questionnaires and working with others to collect data as a team.

Activities menu

1 Produce a wall chart of travel and tourism organisations and their products and services in a destination of your choice either in the UK or abroad.

2 Apply observation and survey approaches from Table 1.5 to collect information about a tourist destination.

3 Research and analyse the travel and tourism experiences and attitudes of stakeholder groups in a destination. The questionnaires in Figure 1.34 and 1.35 can be adapted for your use.

4 *Vocational scenario*
Imagine a tour operator based in another country has employed your services as a consultant. The tour operator specialises in coach tours for retired people. It is considering running tours to a particular destination. Produce a report that evaluates the suitability for its clients of facilities provided by the travel and tourism industry in the destination.

2

Customers: the people thing

2

Customers: the people thing

Starter: **travel and tourism people**

Travel and tourism is a people industry. Travellers and tourists are customers of the industry. People working in the travel and tourism industries provide products and services for customers. Therefore, there is a lot of interaction between people.

Customers

Customers of the travel and tourism industry include members of the travelling public who are tourists and, in the case of some transport providers such as train companies, people who are travelling within their local area to work or for leisure purposes. **Commuters** are people who travel regularly between home and work. They are not tourists but they are still customers of the travel and tourism organisation concerned.

A **customer** is any person or organisation who is provided with a product or service. The customer may pay for the product or service, but this is not always so. Travel and tourism organisations are mostly commercial organisations (see Chapter 1.2), so they aim to make a profit, but they may provide some products or services free to help satisfy customers. For example, a train company may provide information without charge from a help desk at a main railway station. This information will make it easier or more satisfying for the customer to use the company's trains, so they are likely to buy, or to continue to buy, the company's products — train journeys. Of course, good customer service needs to be provided during the journey (Figure 2.1).

Organisations as customers

Customers may be individuals or organisations (corporate customers). For example, a hotel provides conference facilities. A mobile phone company pays for the hire of a room for an all-day meeting, with refreshments and lunch provided. An employee of the phone company

David du Plessis

made the initial booking but the manager hosting the training meeting is another member of staff. Both represent the customer, which is the mobile phone company.

Corporate customers may be other travel and tourism organisations. Imagine a UK tour operator has arranged a package tour for a group of British students to New York. After their arrival at Newark Airport near New York City, a local coach company transfers the group to a Manhattan hotel. As far as the coach company is concerned, the tour operator is its customer, but so is the student party. Since the students are customers of the UK tour operator, they are also customers of the US coach firm.

Figure 2.1
Interactions between travel and tourism people and first-class customers during a train journey

Internal and external customers

Internal customers are people within a travel and tourism organisation who are provided with goods and services by their colleagues as part of the organisation's operations.

People working in the travel and tourism industry spend much of their time working as a team. They provide for each other's needs as well as for those of their external customers. External customers are people from outside the organisation who are having travel and tourism products and services provided.

On an airline, flight refreshments may be provided from a trolley staffed by **cabin crew** — the customer service staff of the company who look after the safety and welfare of passengers during the journey. Working as a team, they make sure that each other's trolleys are kept supplied with what is needed. If one runs out of tea, another member of staff may make sure it is replenished so that the passengers are served efficiently. Equally, a member of the cabin crew may see that the **flight crew** (the pilot and the assistant first officer) receive the refreshments they require on the flight deck. In this scenario, the cabin crew are serving the passengers as external customers and their colleagues and flight crew as internal customers.

The importance of customer service

As a student of travel and tourism, you will learn that good customer service is vital to any travel and tourism organisation. If an organisation does not serve customers well, they may be dissatisfied and not wish to buy products and services from it again.

Customers spend money. Most travel and tourism organisations are commercial businesses whose success relies on taking money from customers and making a profit. Good service makes for satisfied customers who may feel encouraged to spend more, perhaps on a return visit — **repeat business**. At least as important is that they may recommend the organisation to other **potential customers**. Potential customers are people who may become **actual customers** of a travel and tourism organisation such as a travel agency. They are the **target market** at which the organisation aims its promotional activities, including advertising. Recommendations amount to free advertisements for the travel agency. They attract new business and new money without any additional marketing costs, so adding to profits.

Bedroom

Did you find your bedroom clean and welcoming?

| Excellent | 5 | 4 | 3 | 2 | 1 | Poor |

Comments _____

_____

Was the level of bathroom cleanliness to a satisfactory standard?

| Excellent | 5 | 4 | 3 | 2 | 1 | Poor |

Comments _____

_____

Were the equipment and facilities in your room in good working order?

| Excellent | 5 | 4 | 3 | 2 | 1 | Poor |

Comments _____

_____

Figure 2.2
A customer comment card

The opposite is also true. Dissatisfied customers may not only choose not to repeat their spending but may actively dissuade other people from using the travel agency. Such loss of potential custom and reputation can be damaging financially for the organisation. For this reason, it is important that customer dissatisfaction is avoided wherever possible, and when it does occur to ensure that it is identified and dealt with. Travel and tourism organisations carefully monitor the satisfaction levels of customers by a variety of techniques including customer comment cards (Figure 2.2). If their customers are dissatisfied, it is important that the causes are known to management before news of it spreads among potential customers.

Senior managers of travel and tourism organisations recognise the crucial importance of good customer service. Organisations provide **induction** packages and other training for their staff, for example in dealing with customers, product knowledge (see Chapter 2.3) and technical skills (see Chapter 2.5). Service Extraordinaire (see Chapter 2.3) is the name given to a programme adopted by Accor Hotels, which operates the Novotel brand, to develop high-quality customer service delivery by their staff (Figure 2.3).

Novotel UK/Accor UK & Ireland Hotels

Figure 2.3 *Novotel's Service Extraordinaire scheme aims to give high-quality customer service to its customers*

Silent customer service

Providing customer service does not always involve direct person-to-person interaction. For example, at a conference centre delegates may be served a buffet lunch in their meeting room. When the centre's catering staff arrives at the pre-arranged time to set out the food, the presenter of the meeting is addressing delegates who are listening closely. It would be inappropriate for the staff to interrupt, so the buffet lunch is silently and unobtrusively laid out.

In some customer service situations, there may be no one involved immediately at all. Customers at a busy or unstaffed railway station, for example, may be able to buy tickets from a machine (Figure 2.4). Business tourists using UK domestic airlines often prefer to use automatic check-in machines rather than queue with leisure tourists who have luggage to check in. In hotel management, ensuring the

NewsCast

Figure 2.4 *Using an automated ticket machine at a railway station*

clean and well-maintained condition of the building is also good customer service. Customers arriving at a travel and tourism facility may need help to find their way around. At a large visitor attraction like a theme park, a map may be given to each customer.

Signage

Signage is an important element of silent customer service. Customers use well-designed signs to find their way around quickly, saving their own time and the time of facility staff, who can then deal with customer service situations where personal interaction is needed. At the same time, all staff of a travel and tourism facility can expect to have to deal with customers — cleaning staff at theme parks and in hotels are among the most frequently approached by customers seeking information.

Discussion point

Is the customer always right?

Support your learning

Information sources

Learn from your own experiences of good and bad customer service in travel and tourism.

Skills builder

Empathy means placing yourself in another's position. Begin to empathise with travel and tourism organisations as you learn about customer service. Start to judge and think about good customer service from the point of view of the organisation, not as a consumer.

Activities menu

1 For one travel and tourism organisation or facility, describe one example each of:
   a customer service given to an external customer.
   b customer service given to an internal customer.

2 *Vocational scenario*
   Imagine you have a new job at a travel and tourism facility. You are on the way to your first staff training session on customer service, which is going to be run by your manager. Another new recruit expresses the view that this is a waste of your manager's time. Explain why it is not.

3 Research and analyse customer service situations in which people you know have experienced good and bad customer service.

4 Evaluate the quality of customer service given during a travel and tourism experience you have had, such as a holiday, journey or visit to a tourist attraction.

2.1

Principles of customer service

The success of a travel and tourism organisation depends on the quality of its customer service. Selling the organisation's products and services is an important aspect of serving customers. Good quality customer service means that:

- sales, visitor numbers and profits rise
- image and reputation improve
- satisfied customers return, providing repeat business
- customers are less likely to choose competitors, so market share is protected
- customers are more likely to recommend the organisation to other people, so market share is protected

For example, a small tour operator selling self-catering holidays in the countryside presents its properties in a brochure. Figure 2.5 is an extract from such a brochure. Good customer service includes the prompt delivery of the brochure when the customer orders it, an accurate description of the property in the brochure, helpful advice if the customer rings to ask for further details, and efficient processing of the booking. If all goes well, the customer may book again the following year and is likely to tell other people about the experience. Holidays are a favourite conversation topic. People show photographs to friends, relatives and colleagues at work, school or college and share the strengths and weaknesses of their holiday experience. Customers of the tour operator who feel they have been well served are likely to generate new business for the organisation. Word of mouth is a valuable marketing mechanism.

Figure 2.5 A self-catering holiday cottage brochure

Cottage

Accommodation is on one level.
Four steps to front door. Comfortable open plan living/ dining room/kitchen. Large twin bedded room. Shower room/WC. **Services.** Electricity and full oil CH (from owners house) included. Electric fire. Colour TV. Electric cooker. Microwave. Fridge. Electric blankets. Patio with furniture. Off road parking. Shop/PO 3 miles. Pub 1.5 miles. **Duvets with linen and towels.** Sorry no pets. No smoking in cottage please.
Availability. Summer/Winter/Short Breaks.

Northumbria Byways

Dress and attitude

Personal appearance and attitude are highly valued for those people in a travel and tourism organisation who come into direct contact with the public.

Dress

Travel and tourism staff often conform to a smart dress code or wear a uniform. This is because:

- Staff are quickly identifiable when the customer needs assistance — this is especially important in a busy space such as a hotel entrance foyer, an airport or railway station or in a visitor attraction such as a theme park. In a travel agency, uniforms distinguish staff from other customers, avoiding possible embarrassment through misidentification (Figure 2.6).
- Smart appearance gives a positive image — it is important to an organisation that customers perceive its staff as being efficient and professional.
- Roles of staff and different levels of seniority can be judged by customers. For example, the duty manager of a hotel may wear a suit, the conference manager a stylishly cut and detailed uniform, and a member of the maintenance or cleaning staff a practical set of looser-cut work clothes. The customer can easily judge whom to approach.

©Photofusion Picture Library/Alamy

Figure 2.6 *Travel agency staff wear a uniform*

The degree of formality chosen for a uniform is part of an organisation's marketing. Trailfinders is a travel agency specialising in tailor-made holidays for independently minded travellers. A relatively informal uniform is judged to be more in keeping with this target market — more likely to put customers at ease with a relaxed first impression, encouraging them to approach staff, which is important if sales are to be achieved.

Fashion-consciousness can sometimes play a part. If the organisation has a target market of young people (teenagers or younger adults), staff uniforms may be more up to date and relatively informal. A junior resort representative working in a children's club needs to be dressed in a way that makes him or her easily identifiable to children, that is practical for play activities, conveys a message of efficiency and maturity to parents while seeming fashionable enough to the children to come over as young and fun to be with.

Other aspects of appearance also matter. Uniforms are only smart when worn correctly; unfastened ties can create an image of slovenliness, for example. Grooming and hygiene are other considerations, not only for health and safety reasons but also because of their significance in how customers perceive staff.

Positive attitude

Customers value a 'can-do' approach. This is where staff have a positive attitude in dealing with clients. Wanting to help people is a state of mind valued by many travel and tourism organisation managers. The right attitude in a potential team member is often judged to be more important for their selection than any skills and knowledge they may have. Staff can be trained by the organisation so that they develop product knowledge and technical skills. Positive attitude is often seen as an inherent quality that cannot be learned.

Meeting customer needs

People who can recognise and meet the needs of other people provide the highest quality customer service.

Providing information is a key function of customer service. This does not necessarily involve the provision of service by personal contact with the customer. The use of signage is an example. Figure 2.7 shows a large screen display directing business tourists on their arrival at a conference centre. In a hotel, where a business conference is being hosted, other examples of when person-to-person contact may not be necessary or appropriate include making sure that:

- the meeting room is air-conditioned to the correct temperature
- appropriate disabled access is provided
- a buffet lunch is served without interruption to the meeting

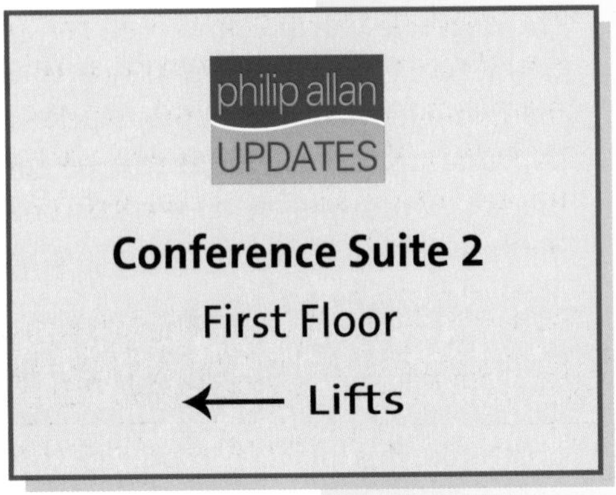

Good customer service is when customers are happy that their needs and expectations have been met, and the travel and tourism organisation has benefited too. Excellent customer service is when customers feel that their expectations have been more than fulfilled. However, this has to be achieved in line with the organisation's customer service policy to the benefit to the organisation. Upgrading a customer on check-in from a standard to an executive room in a hotel or from an economy class to a business class seat on an airliner may mean that the customer's expectations have been exceeded, but check-in staff cannot always offer these services — it depends on availability. Some customers asking for an upgrade will be disappointed, although sensitive handling of such requests can clearly deliver better customer service than if they are turned down brusquely.

philip allan
UPDATES

Conference Suite 2

First Floor

← **Lifts**

Figure 2.7 An example of signage at a conference

Dissatisfaction

If customers feel their expectations are not being met, they may or may not complain. Whether they complain or not, it is a cause for concern for a travel and tourism manager. The uncomplaining dissatisfied customer leaves the facility with the capacity to harm the organisation by expressing dissatisfaction to other people who may be put off the organisation and spread the word even further. The manager may prefer to have heard the complaint so that the cause of the dissatisfaction can be addressed and, if it is of benefit to the company, removed. It is for this reason that travel and tourism organisations survey the customers' opinions about the service they have received. Customer comment cards (see Figure 2.2 on page 63) are commonly used by organisations such as hotels.

On the other hand, when customers do complain it may be difficult to fulfil or exceed their expectations. Many travel and tourism organisations would expect a senior staff member or manager to deal with direct customer complaints. This is partly because their greater experience of dealing with people may lead to a more skilful resolution of the situation and partly because they may have more authority to make the customer an offer to compensate for some failing in service.

Figure 2.8
A dissatisfied customer scenario

Scenario: a provincial airport check-in desk. A customer approaches the desk with a computer print-out confirming a booking ticket for the next flight to London Heathrow.

David du Plessis

Figure 2.8 shows a fictional interchange between a customer and staff members in a situation in which the customer's expectations were initially disappointed. The strengths of the service the customer received are that as far as the customer was concerned, he was spoken to politely, kept informed about what the difficulty was, discretely referred to a member of staff with the technical skills to deal with the issue, and the matter was resolved quickly at no extra cost to him. From the organisation's point of view, only one ticket was issued and that has been paid for, so the company has not lost out financially. The report sent by the sales team member will allow management to review what, if anything, went wrong with its systems in producing the mystery cancellation in order to stop any repeat instances.

However, the customer perceives something went wrong with his online booking and that may deter him from booking with the airline again in the future. Some follow-up action may therefore be advisable.

Evaluating customer service quality is important to travel and tourism organisations. This is explained in more detail in Chapter 2.6. One approach taken, for example, by Accor Hotels is floor-walking. Senior staff or the staff training coach walk around the hotel on a daily basis observing customer service and reporting their observations to the managers of different departments in the hotel, such as the front-of-house department that includes reception and reservations.

Spreading good practice

The effective travel and tourism manager also wants to know about and reward members of staff whose customer service has been particularly appreciated by clients. Hotels and other organisations may include a question on their customer comment card asking if any member of staff has given outstanding service. Figure 2.9 shows an example of a tool that customers can use to provide positive feedback.

The manager can facilitate the spread of good practice among the staff as part of on-going staff training and development. Staff team members may be invited to act as coaches for colleagues, or more informally be encouraged to share examples of their work at staff meetings. For example, a staff team member mentioned on forms such as the one in Figure 2.9 may be congratulated and asked to explain to other team members what it was that he/she has done.

Figure 2.9
A customer feedback form

Date _____

Team member's name _____

Comments _____

_____

_____

_____

_____

_____

_____

Guest's name _____

Room number _____

Badges

It is common in travel and tourism for members of staff to wear identifying badges with their first or preferred name so that customers can identify them. Such badges may also use flag devices to show which languages the staff member can use. Figure 2.10 illustrates a typical badge. Sometimes the flag of the country in which the organisation is located may be omitted because clients will assume staff speak its language. In facilities with an international customer base, such as Disneyland, cast members (as staff there are known) may themselves be from a variety of countries, each capable of dealing with customers in several languages. It can be reassuring for incoming tourists to see a badge with a flag representing their own language.

Figure 2.10 An example of a staff badge

Support your learning

Information sources

1 Many people have been travel and tourism industry customers. They are a valuable source of experiences.

2 Travel and tourism organisations may provide examples of dress codes and customer comment cards or questionnaires. Managers may be willing to explain the rationale behind them, if approached by your teacher.

3 The websites of travel and tourism organisations often include pages about the customer service they deliver.

Skills builder

Role play. Devise some travel and tourism customer service scenarios and practise them with a partner.

Activities menu

1 Make a list of factors that make up good customer service and explain each one.

2 Suggest and justify two appropriate customer service actions that airline or check-in staff may have taken to follow up the scenario shown in Figure 2.9.

3 Talk to people you know to research and analyse examples of travel and tourism customer service they have received.

4 *Vocational scenario*
Imagine you are a staff training coach in a travel and tourism facility and you have observed instances of customer service. Evaluate the strengths and weaknesses of the customer service you have observed. This may have been a role-play simulation.

2.2

Internal and external customers

Internal customers are the people served within a travel and tourism organisation. Employees of a company provide for the needs of other staff who are their internal customers. For example, in a travel agency a member of staff may be delegated to deal with foreign exchange, providing foreign currency for a travel consultant colleague (the internal customer) to pass on to clients.

External customers are people from outside an organisation whom it serves. They may be individual members of the public or another organisation. In the example above, the travel consultant's clients are the external customers. They may be members of the public who have booked a holiday abroad or another travel and tourism organisation such as a coach company providing a tour abroad. External customers that are organisations need not necessarily be part of the travel and tourism industry. For example, a marketing manager of a manufacturer may travel to the USA on company business. In this business tourism example, the external customer organisation is the manufacturing company.

Situations

Customer service situations involving both internal and external customers arise in travel and tourism organisations belonging to all six sectors of the industry.

Case study: Village Holidays

Village Holidays is a small tour operator. The business specialises in arranging self-catering holidays to Provence (southern France). Typically, potential customers respond to small classified advertisements placed by Village Holidays in the travel sections of weekend

> ### *Village Holidays*
>
> Self-catering gîtes in Provence.
> Ferry crossings, overnight hotels, Motorail available.
> Ring now (24 hours) for free colour brochure.
>
> *Contact details...*

Figure 2.11 *An extract from a Village Holidays newspaper advert*

newspaper supplements. Figure 2.11 shows an extract from one of its advertisements.

Contact details include a 24-hour telephone number (connected to an answering machine out of office hours) and an e-mail address. Potential customers order a brochure, which is posted to them. Having studied the brochure, external customers may ring Village Holidays and either make further enquiries about one of the self-catering properties they have seen in the brochure (an example is shown in Figure 2.12) or make a booking. The tour operator at Village Holidays takes the external customer's details, asks him/her to complete a booking form (Figure 2.13) and puts together a holiday package.

For an independent traveller, this package may simply be the self-catering accommodation in the Provence countryside. However, many customers take advantage of package deals including travel and/or en-route accommodation at prices cheaper than they may be if they booked these components of their holiday separately.

Elements of a typical Village Holidays package are:

- accommodation in a self-catering gîte
- ferry crossing from the UK for a car and passengers
- overnight stay in a hotel en route or Motorail transfer from Calais to Avignon

BD6 This property is situated 800 m from Bedoin and is overlooked by Mont Ventoux. Inside are a living room with beamed ceiling, and a well-fitted kitchen including washing machine and shower room. There is a twin bedroom and a double bed on the wooden mezzanine.

©PCL/Alamy

Outside is a large private pool terrace, open space and parking.

Sleeps 4

Price group A

Figure 2.12 *A self-catering property from the Village Holidays brochure*

Booking Form   *Village Holidays*

1. Your name and address (to which all correspondence will be sent):

Name _____

Address _____

_____

_____

Postcode _____

Telephone (including dialling code): Day_____ Evening _____

e-mail: Day _____ Evening _____

Please tell us where you saw our advert or how you heard about us

_____

2. Your property and your party

Property reference code	From	To	Adults	Children (state ages)

Sometimes accommodation may already be booked, so it would be helpful to give us a second, or even third, choice.

3. Your ferry crossing

	From	To	Date	Preferred time
Outward				
Return				

Extra passengers (your first week price includes the first 2 adults):

Adults (14 years and over):   _____   £ _____

Children (4–13 years):   _____   £ _____

Children under 4 years: _____   FREE

Figure 2.13
Village Holidays booking form

Motorail trains carry cars and passengers on long overland journeys of several hundred kilometres. In France, Village Holidays customers travel overnight and have sleeping accommodation on the train.

External customer service situations

Two partners run the Village Holidays tour operator business. One is a fluent French speaker. When customers book a gîte, the French-speaking partner liaises with the owner in France. Gîtes are self-catering cottages and apartments in the French countryside owned by local people. Village Holidays acts as a booking agency for these

Before UK customer's holiday	
UK tourist clients	**French property owner**
• Telephone/e-mail brochure request. • Post brochure. • Telephone/e-mail further details request. Discussion. • Telephone/e-mail provisional booking request. Take deposit (if debit/credit card). • Post/fax booking form and deposit (debit/credit card details/cheque). • Booking confirmed by telephone/e-mail. • Post balance payment reminder. • Receive balance payment. • Discuss arrival time and final details with UK client, usually by telephone. • Post Village Holidays holiday pack with property address, ferry/Motorail tickets, hotel stay voucher and customer evaluation form.	• Inspect property and agree price face to face with French owner (previous summer). Take photographs. • Telephone/e-mail UK client booking details. • Post written confirmation of UK client booking details. • Transfer payments, usually by post (cheque). • Telephone/e-mail UK client's arrival time. Arrange for French owner to greet UK clients.
After UK customer's holiday	
• Receive customer evaluation form and act on any comments or complaints. • Send next year's brochure to client's address.	• Post copy of customer evaluation comments. • Telephone to discuss customer comments and arrange next inspection visit.

Table 2.1 Village Holidays external customer service situations

people, selling accommodation for them on the UK travel and tourism market. As Table 2.1 shows, both the French owners and the UK clients are external customers of Village Holidays. The table also lists customer service situations that arise in dealings with both sets of their external customers.

Village Holidays is an external customer of the transport and accommodation providers with which it deals. Two organisations that have featured in Village Holidays brochures are French Railways (providers of Motorail transfers) and Mercure Hotels (providers of overnight hotel accommodation for clients driving through France). Most of the customer service situations in this context take the form of telephone calls, faxes and e-mail and letter exchanges between Village Holidays and the provider. For example, the tour operator at Village Holidays telephones French Railways to make the booking. Written confirmation of the booking and payment and tickets are sent through the post.

WTM Picture Library

Figure 2.14 *The World Travel Market in London*

In addition, there are face-to-face customer service situations. Village Holidays receives visits from representatives of the suppliers marketing their organisation's products and services. The partners also receive **corporate hospitality** from these organisations at trade fairs such as the **World Travel Market** held annually in London.

The World Travel Market

The World Travel Market (Figure 2.14) is a large travel trade fair held in the autumn where travel and tourism organisations from the industry worldwide assemble to market their products and services, mostly to each other. Organisations involved in domestic, inbound and outbound tourism in the UK are represented. Corporate hospitality is a marketing tool employed by travel and tourism organisations. It involves entertaining external customers, without charge, with a variety of perks (or treats) ranging from drinks to tickets to an event such as a sporting fixture. Visitor attractions such as major sporting venues or racecourses often organise corporate hospitality facilities such as **private boxes** for businesses to entertain their customers. A private box is a small, enclosed area of seating in a stadium or theatre where customers can sit apart from the general audience and often have special catering arranged for them.

Support services

Village Holidays deals with a variety of organisations that may be classified as support services. Some are purely travel and tourism organisations that belong entirely to the support services sector of the UK travel and tourism industry. Others provide support for Village Holidays just as they would for any other small enterprise. In this latter category come organisations providing Village Holidays with support services, including:

- credit card payment facilities
- banking
- accountancy
- office equipment and supplies
- design and printing of brochure and promotional materials
- advertising

Travel Insurance Services is a specialist provider of insurance support that Village Holidays uses to offer its tourist customers the option of taking out travel insurance. In this way, Village Holidays has acted as an agent for the insurance company (Travel Insurance Services).

Internal customer service situations

Figure 2.15 shows customer service processes within Village Holidays as one partner deals with the other. Situations are mostly face to face but also involve telephone calls as, for example, external customer booking requests or gîte availability information is transferred within Village Holidays between the partners.

In a larger organisation, there are likely to be more internal customer service situations. For example, in a hotel such as the Novotel York in Figure 2.16, one role undertaken by front-of-house staff is to host business tourist delegates to conferences (see Chapter 2.3).

Front of house

The front-of-house department of the hotel is the section that deals directly with external customers, making reservations and performing reception duties including answering enquiries and arranging guest check-in and check-out. Staff in the kitchen belong to the food and beverage department and may not have much direct external customer contact. The same may apply to members of the maintenance department. However, external customer service situations do arise, for example when undertaking a repair in a guest's room or when approached by a

> Steve takes provisional booking of property BD6 by telephone. He writes a memo for Deborah.

> Deborah reads the external customer details memo from Steve and provides the service of telephoning the owner in Bedoin to check the property's availability and to place the booking with him.

> Deborah passes the confirmation of the booking to Steve so he can confirm it with the external customer.

Figure 2.15
Village Holidays internal customer service flowchart

Figure 2.16 *The Novotel York*

guest with a query. Customer service can involve any member of staff. Employees belonging to the housekeeping department, which is involved in room cleaning, are among staff most frequently approached by the hotel's external customers.

An internal customer scenario

Conference organiser Victoria dealt with a network of internal customers on behalf of a business organisation client, during a 1-day business meeting at the hotel (Figure 2.17). A meeting room had been booked in advance for 20 business tourist delegates, but Victoria learned that morning that there were to be only 5. They were to have refreshments provided throughout the day for breaks during the meeting and would lunch in the restaurant.

> **Discussion point** ⦿
>
> Is internal customer service less important in a small enterprise such as Village Holidays than in a larger facility such as a Novotel Hotel?

Figure 2.17 *Victoria's network of internal customers*

Airport customer service situations

Airports, such as Newcastle International Airport (Figure 2.18), are managed by travel and tourism organisations belonging to the transport providers sector of the travel and tourism industry. However, they are places where a number of organisations belonging to different sectors of the travel and tourism industry provide customer service to their tourist clients. In a regional airport terminal building such as at Newcastle, there are likely to be airline sales and check-in desks, car hire firm counters, retail and catering outlets, ATM cash machines and an airport information desk.

freefoto.com

Figure 2.18
Newcastle
International Airport

Travel and tourism organisations with a presence at the airport provide customer service for each other and for the airport's management company, Newcastle International Airport Ltd. Most of the people working at Newcastle Airport are not employees of Newcastle International Airport Ltd, but work instead for the terminal retail and catering outlet companies and for the ground-handling companies Groundstar and Servisair, which operate there providing services such as check-in and baggage handling.

Customers of Newcastle International Airport Ltd include airlines such as British Airways, Air France and easyJet, for whom the airport provides landing rights and terminal facilities. Groundstar and Servisair provide aircraft handling services like refuelling.

Employees belonging to any one of the organisations operating at the airport provide internal customer service for each other. However, much of the customer service delivered at the airport is to external customers. This is because, apart from leisure, business and VFR tourist customers, each organisation (Newcastle Airport Ltd, airlines, Servisair, retail and catering firms) is a separate enterprise. Therefore, even though they all operate at the airport, they are external customers for each other. The airlines, for example, are external customers of Newcastle International Airport Ltd and of the ground-handling organisations that provide them with support services.

Priorities

In a customer service situation such as a reception desk, external and internal customers may be waiting to be served. As an example scenario, a staff member waiting at the reception desk is concluding a telephone call with a customer when two other people approach the desk. First to arrive is a staff colleague and then, almost immediately afterwards, an external customer approaches the desk. Normal practice is not to follow 'first come, first served', but to deal with the external customer first. External customers are a source of revenue for the company and so their satisfaction is the immediate priority.

The internal customer may be making an enquiry on behalf of a client. If she is the conference manager, she may be seeking a missing piece of equipment for a conference presenter, but she will have been trained to deal with the slight delay with her customer when she returns to the conference suite of the hotel.

Customers are people that travel and tourism organisations provide with products and services. External customers often include members of the public and are from outside the organisations, like tourists. Internal customers are other people from within the organisation — other members of staff. Staff of travel and tourism organisations are still classified as external customers, even though they work within the industry.

Support your learning

Information sources

Travel and tourism organisations from all six sectors are likely to have internal and external customer service situations. A visit or contact with their management is a potential information source.

Skills builder

A work placement in a travel and tourism organisation or a work-shadowing opportunity will help you practise or observe skills of customer service that are transferable to other travel and tourism customer service scenarios.

Activities menu

1 Identify situations where you have been served as an external customer by staff of travel and tourism organisations.

2 For the situations you identified in Activity 1, suggest the internal customer service that would be needed to support the external customer service you received. For example, if you were served a meal on an aircraft, what internal customer service situations lie behind that provision?

3 *Vocational scenario*
Imagine a customer service consultancy from outside the travel and tourism industry has been commissioned to report on the contribution made by internal customer service to the overall customer service that travel and tourism organisations provide.

You have been engaged by the consultancy to examine a facility in the transport providers' sector of the industry. Visit a large transport-providing facility such as an airport terminal building or mainline railway station. Research and analyse customer service situations there. Classify your observations as external or internal and by their nature, i.e. face-to-face, telephone or electronic communication.

4 Evaluate the contribution made by internal customer service to the overall customer service of one travel and tourism organisation or facility.

2.3

Induction and training in travel and tourism

A travel and tourism organisation's staff provide customer service. The managements of travel and tourism organisations want to make sure staff deliver high-quality customer service. Therefore, staff training and **induction** are vital. Induction is the introductory phase of training when a new staff member is acquainted with the organisation and its procedures. Good practice by travel and tourism managers is to ensure that staff training is ongoing so that employees are up to date and fresh in their customer service delivery.

Case study: Novotel hotels

Induction procedures and training provided by Novotel hotels are part of the Accor Hotels group Service Extraordinaire programme.

Accor Hotels is the **parent company** of Novotel. Novotel is an international hotel chain that originated in France and has 30 hotels in the UK. A parent company is a large business that owns at least one other organisation.

'Service Extraordinaire' means 'extraordinary service'. It is a programme aimed at involving hotel staff in providing excellent customer service. The first Novotel hotel to introduce Service Extraordinaire was Novotel London West in 2003. That year, Novotel London West won the Best Training Team of the Year award for Service Excellence in the National Consumer Service Awards.

Novotel has defined the customer service it wants its guests to enjoy. This is presented in Figure 2.19. The organisation's management came to

Figure 2.19
An extract from Novotel's Service Extraordinaire staff handbook

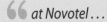

" *at Novotel . . .*
I have a hassle-free stay
Staff are proactive in meeting my needs
I feel comfortable and relaxed
I have a choice in the service I receive
Service is delivered with a human touch "

this definition largely by analysing research it had conducted among its guests (external customers), as well as by collecting the views of its staff (internal customers). Service Extraordinaire aims to deliver the response shown in Figure 2.19 from Novotel's customers. Novotel formed a partnership with an external organisation, Mary Gober International, to help launch the Service Extraordinaire customer service project.

Induction

Induction is the process of introducing new staff to the hotel (or any travel and tourism organisation). On their first day, new employees receive a presentation from the Novotel General Manager about the Accor Hotels organisation. They meet their head of department — the senior member of staff in charge of the section of the hotel where they will be working. Figure 2.20 shows the management structure of the Novotel York. The Novotel York has 124 bedrooms (Figure 2.21), making it a relatively small hotel for a Novotel in the UK. The hotel has a fairly

Figure 2.20 Novotel York's management structure

Figure 2.21 One of the Novotel York's bedrooms

'flat structure', which means staff work as a team on a relatively equal basis. Some are more senior than others (the general manager is in charge of the department managers, who in turn manage their own team members), but there is less separation of staff by status than in a more hierarchical structure where there are more distinct levels of status.

Larger hotels, including others in the UK Novotel network, may have more management roles, such as a rooms division manager or an operations manager to act as a deputy for the general manager.

The head of department arranges for the new recruits to meet the other members of the department team, explains their job role and shows them the kind of career progression they might expect if they are successful in that role.

Each member of Novotel's staff agrees to keep up the four key hotel standards shown in Figure 2.22. All the staff are trained in these four standards and the seven service behaviours shown in Figure 2.23. This training is delivered in one 3-hour session.

This induction training is given to all employees of Novotel and to any regular agency staff that may be employed in one of its hotels. Hotels may use other organisations that supply experienced staff to work in hotels on a short-term basis as and when a hotel needs them because of a staffing shortfall or because it is going to be particularly busy and needs to take on extra people for a while.

Training

The Novotel York has joined the Service Extraordinaire programme. The hotel's existing staff were trained in Service Extraordinaire by:

- Awareness raising: staff meetings, posters in the hotel and newsletters were used to familiarise them with the four hotel standards (Figure 2.22).
- Induction to Service Extraordinaire: because this was a new programme, all staff attended the 3-hour induction course.
- Hotel employees who were already used to dealing with customers attending a 2-day **seminar**: a seminar is a training meeting held among a relatively small group of people (usually less than 20) who discuss issues with each other and with the leader of the seminar, who chairs the meeting.

Figure 2.22 *The four hotel standards*

1. Look professional — be professional
2. Greet every guest and colleague
3. Look after your hotel
4. Be positive

Figure 2.23
The seven service standards

1. Be positive
2. Be gracious
3. Be a listener
4. Be a communicator
5. Be solution-orientated
6. Be responsible
7. Be thankful

Service behaviour 1

BE POSITIVE
and give your guests confidence first time, every time

Group 2

Scenario	Typical response	Correct response
I don't have any towels in my room.	OK, I'll get some sent up for you.	Thank you for bringing this to my attention. I'm sorry for any inconvenience caused to you. I'll ensure that some towels are brought up to your room immediately.
Thank you for your help.	No problem!	It's my pleasure!
Can you tell me where the Tower Conference Room is?	Just over there, sir.	Certainly, sir. Let me show you where it is.
Hello. I'd like to check in please.	Yes, madam. Can I have your reservation number please?	Certainly, madam. Welcome to Novotel Central. May I ask your full name, please?
Can I have a pen, please?	Yes, there you are.	Certainly, I'll bring one to you straight away.
Can I book a table for dinner, please?	Yes, sir. For what time?	Certainly. What time would suit you, sir?

Service Extraordinaire training includes a presentation, a video, role plays and group discussion of customer service scenarios, including transcripts of face-to-face situations and dealing with telephone messages and letters from external customers. Figure 2.24 is an example of some training material, contrasting 'typical' hotel staff responses with the expected Novotel 'correct' responses.

Figure 2.24
A Novotel training scenario

Hotel coaches

Figure 2.25 is an extract from the Novotel Service Extraordinaire staff handbook that explains the role of hotel coach.

Hotel coaches need not be senior members of the hotel management. They are simply established members of the team who have an interest in and an aptitude for developing the customer service skills of their colleagues. When the hotel coach system was

Discussion point ●

Why are the 'correct' responses better customer service?

SERVICE EXTRAORDINAIRE™ — THE COACHES

MEET OUR COACHES

Oana-Maria V. Stoicescu
MICE Operations

What is the role of the Hotel Coach?

Those members of the team who show an aptitude for providing Service Extraordinaire™ and who want to coach their colleagues can apply to become Service Extraordinaire™ Coaches. Coaches are selected solely on the basis of their attitude and behaviour.

Our coaches are essential players in this project and ensure that skills learnt in the classroom are transferred to the workplace. It is important to remember that they coach as part of their everyday working life and support the Management Team and employees, ensuring that events, activities and the actions happen across the hotel, regardless of the department or function.

The coaches receive training in the delivery of the Service Extraordinaire™ half-day introduction. They then attend an intensive 'Train the Coach' programme under the guidance of an external consultancy to enable them to coach their colleagues who have attended the 2-day 'Language of Service' seminar.

MEET OUR COACHES

Carole Sibuet
Bars

NOVOTEL
ACCOR hotels

first introduced at the Novotel York, two senior managers were the first hotel coaches, but they identified staff who had skills and qualities to become coaches themselves. Hotel coaches are able to pass on comments that help colleagues keep up the four hotel standards without it seeming like a reprimand from a manager. For example, one of the standards is to look professional. A team member who is not looking as smart or as well groomed as usual may feel less threatened to have this pointed out by a peer than by a senior manager. Standards in the hotel are such, however, that staff can expect such comments.

Product knowledge

Product knowledge is the set of facts a staff member needs to learn about the travel and tourism product he/she is serving to customers.

Figure 2.25 An extract from the Novotel Service Extraordinaire staff handbook

Discussion point

Is the hotel coach system a good approach to keeping customer service standards high?

In the Novotel York, all product knowledge training is delivered in house. This means staff are trained in what they need to know at work in the hotel by colleagues including one of the hotel coaches.

The general manager places more emphasis on attitude than prior product knowledge when selecting new junior staff for the hotel. The most important criterion is a positive attitude shown by an enthusiastic, confident (but not excessively extrovert) manner. Successful applicants should also demonstrate a caring and patient approach. It is all about having an attitude of wanting to be of service others, leading to a sense of fulfilment from having helped the hotel's customers, both external and internal.

In the front-of-house department, for example, staff are trained to know about the range of facilities and services offered by the hotel (Table 2.2), so that they can work in reception, greeting customers, arranging check-in and check-out, answering customer requests face

Facilities	Services
Rooms	◆ 124 en-suite bedrooms with dressing table/workstation (desk and modem point for internet access), direct-dial telephone, remote control satellite television, pay movies and pay PlayStation, tea- and coffee-making facilities, blackout curtains and hairdryer ◆ Four bedrooms suitable for disabled access ◆ 62 bedrooms able to accommodate families of up to two adults and two children ◆ Room service menu
Public areas	◆ Reception ◆ Room and conference reservation ◆ Drinks, snacks and light meals in the Old Glassworks Pub inside the hotel ◆ Restaurant meals in the Garden Brasserie for breakfast, lunch and dinner
Meeting rooms	◆ Rendezvous meeting and conference suite ◆ Five ground-floor rooms that can be subdivided to accommodate conference and business meeting groups from 8 to 210 people in one space ◆ Air conditioning, natural daylight and blackout curtains ◆ Conference staff support ◆ Catering
Leisure facilities	◆ Swimming pool ◆ Outdoor children's play area
Car parking	◆ 150 free spaces for hotel residents

Table 2.2 *Facilities and services of the Novotel York*

1. On reception.

Good morning, sir.

Hello. What's on the special menu you're advertising for tomorrow night? I have a wheat allergy — will there be a good choice for me?

Right, sir, I understand. I'll print off a copy of the menu for you, and I'll just check with the kitchen.

2. In the kitchen the telephone rings.

Hello, kitchen. Angelo speaking.

Good morning, Angelo. This is Sarah on reception. I've a guest asking about wheat-free dishes on tomorrow night's special menu. I can see some, but I'm not sure about all of them. I wonder if you can help us out.

OK, Sarah. I'll come along if you like.

That would be great, Angelo. I'll let the gentleman know you're coming.

3. Back in reception, Angelo arrives.

Hello, sir. I see Sarah's got you a copy of tomorrow night's special menu. Shall we take a seat? I'll go through it with you and point out the wheat-free options. If there's something particular you would like, I'm sure we can sort something out.

David du Plessis

to face and by telephone, and providing for customer needs — for example, calling for a taxi. Members of the front-of-house team, however, are also expected to be able to deal with reservations so that they can move seamlessly from one role to another and back.

External customers expect reception staff to answer questions about facilities and services provided by the hotel, and their prices, as well as those provided by other travel and tourism organisations in York. As well as knowing about the Garden Brasserie Restaurant in the hotel, they need to be able to give advice to guests wanting to eat out in the town centre. A local geography of York and the surrounding area is necessary for staff to be able to give directions to customers who ask for them.

Internal customers expect colleagues to be able to help them so they in turn can help the hotel guests. One example of this would be if a hotel guest enquires about the menu for the next day and the ingredients of a particular dish because he/she is concerned about an allergy. The reception desk staff member would not be expected by the hotel management to have intimate product knowledge such as this, but would be able to ring the kitchen and expect one of the chefs to provide the answer. In an ideal situation, a chef may have the time to come out of the kitchen and discuss the issue with the guest directly.

Figure 2.26
A product knowledge and customer scenario

As far as the hotel's management is concerned, what matters is that external customers are pleased with the service they receive. This means either that staff have sufficient product knowledge to answer a query themselves or that they know who else on the team to contact. If they become the internal customer of the expert staff member, they have a right to expect to receive good product knowledge so that they can pass the information on to the external customer. Figure 2.26 illustrates this in practice.

Discussion point

To what extent is the Novotel York providing customer service to business tourists?

Support your learning

Information sources

Staff induction and training programmes are provided by travel and tourism organisations in all sectors of the industry. Organisations locally, including larger organisations with local facilities, may be able to provide information including examples of their materials.

Skills builder

1 Work-based learning. A work placement in a travel and tourism organisation would help equip you with customer service skills and see induction from the inside.

2 Role play. Practise customer service scenarios such as those in this chapter.

Activities menu

1 *Vocational scenario*
   Imagine that you are a staff trainer in a travel and tourism organisation belonging to another sector of the industry. You have been asked to find out about the induction and staff training programmes in other organisations. Provide your manager with the summary she has requested of Novotel's practice.

2 Devise training materials like the scenario in Figure 2.24 for a travel and tourism organisation in another sector of the industry.

3 Research and analyse the product knowledge required of the holder of a travel and tourism job of your choice. Your analysis should include any customer service demands placed on that knowledge.

4 Evaluate the benefits to customer service of the staff induction and training programme of a travel and tourism organisation.

2.4

Delivering customer service

Customer service situations

In travel and tourism organisations, different customer service situations arise. Staff may deal with customers:

- face to face
- on the telephone
- via written communication, such as letter or e-mail

Travel and tourism professionals also need to respond to messages on answerphones and in written form such as customer comment cards, as well as on standardised booking forms like the one in Figure 2.13 (see Chapter 2.2).

Different customers

Customers may be external to the organisation (see Chapter 2.2), such as members of the public or client organisations, or they may be internal colleagues.

Travel and tourism organisations may have dealings with a wide variety of customers:

- from different age groups
- from different social and cultural backgrounds
- with different income levels
- with special needs

The size of customer group may vary. In a hotel, for example, newly arriving customers will range from single customers or couples to family groups or large coach parties. Some customers are more pleasant and amenable than others. A well-trained travel and tourism staff member will deal with all customers politely, professionally and efficiently. This includes customers who are dissatisfied as well as those who are satisfied by service they have received. Dealing with complaining customers is part of delivering customer service.

Examples of practical scenarios of dealing with different customer types in different situations in all six sectors of the travel and tourism industry are given in Chapter 2.6.

Customers with special needs

It can be argued that any need of the customer is special as it is likely to seem special to the customer at the time. However, travel and tourism managers see customer special needs as those that are particular to certain customer groups. These groups include:

- customers with mobility needs (such as wheelchair users)
- those who are sight- or hearing-impaired
- parents with very young children (toddlers and babies)
- in the UK, customers such as inbound tourists who are not fluent in English (or Welsh)

Figure 2.27 Washroom facilities adapted for special needs

Customer service that addresses these needs includes facility provision as well as interaction with staff. In other words, it is not just a matter of training staff to communicate in particular ways but also of ensuring that special facilities and services are available. Figure 2.27 shows an example.

The British Museum is a major visitor attraction in London. The management of the museum has made a number of special needs provisions. Figure 2.28 is a plan of the main (ground) floor of the museum. Symbols on the plan and in its key show a number of provisions aimed at customers with special needs. These include:

- toilets accessible to wheelchair users in four locations on the main floor of the museum
- babycare facilities in three locations on the main floor, including nappy changing and feeding
- **audio tours** available in several languages and for children

Courtesy of GNER

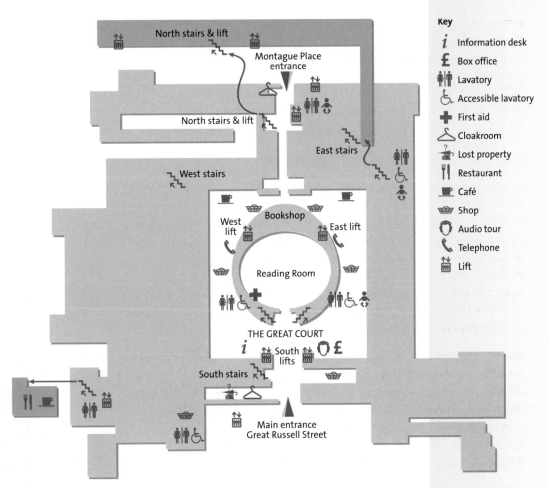

Key

i	Information desk
£	Box office
🚹🚺	Lavatory
♿	Accessible lavatory
✚	First aid
🧥	Cloakroom
	Lost property
🍴	Restaurant
☕	Café
🛒	Shop
🎧	Audio tour
☎	Telephone
🛗	Lift

Figure 2.28 Main floor plan of the British Museum showing special needs provision

Audio tours are recorded information about an attraction played back to a customer. The customer hires a replay device, usually with an accompanying map or plan of the attraction — typically a museum, art gallery or historical monument such as a castle or cathedral. These tours may be provided with a telephone-type device that allows visitors to dial up the number of a particular exhibit and to listen to a recorded message about it.

Other special needs provisions at the British Museum include:

- Access: wheelchair loan and designated pre-bookable car parking spaces for disabled visitors, magnifying glass loan and object-handling by appointment for visitors with visual impairment, sign-interpreted tours and hearing enhancement induction loops.
- Children and families: highchairs to use in the cafés, children's tours and a school holiday picnic space.

Some facilities, such as lifts and seating areas, potentially benefit all customers but also add value to the provision that has been made for customers with special needs, such as elderly visitors who may not find it easy to climb stairs or to stand and walk for long periods. Lifts are valuable mobility aids in any facility on more than one floor for a number of customer groups including wheelchair users, family groups with pushchairs and anyone whose walking ability is limited in some way.

The importance of customer service

Customer service matters to travel and tourism organisations because they depend on their external customers for survival and prosperity. External customers spend money that adds up to the turnover of the company. In addition, external customers are in contact with other people who may be potential customers of the organisation. They spread news of their experience of the organisation's customer service. Such good (and bad) news fuels the reputation of the organisation and this affects how much business it does. Satisfied customers are more likely to return and generate repeat business.

Internal customer service matters too. The better it is, the more efficient and smooth-running the travel and tourism organisation is. Good internal customer service makes for more contented employees, which in turn contributes to efficiency. Efficient travel and tourism organisations are those that are most successful.

Prioritisation

In a travel and tourism organisation, staff may need to prioritise the order in which they deal with customers. As explained in Chapter 2.2, it is normal practice that external customers take priority over internal customers.

Customers are generally understanding if they need to wait while another person is served, but queues can lead to customer dissatisfaction. Queue management strategies can mitigate this risk by providing information about the wait, providing designated areas (such as waiting rooms at railway stations) or by reducing waiting times. At visitor attractions such as theme parks, there can be long waits for rides. A common strategy is to put up signs giving the waiting time, e.g. '30 minutes from here', from certain points in the queue line.

At airports, check-in waiting times are reduced by strategies such as express queues for passengers not travelling economy class and

Topfoto

Figure 2.29 A customer using a self check-in machine

automatic check-in machines for business tourists who may not have luggage for the aircraft hold and do not wish to be held in a queue by holidaymakers with baggage to check in (Figure 2.29).

Skills for travel and tourism people

Travel and tourism organisations that are successful provide good customer service. They recognise that staff need to develop their skills in dealing with customers and have staff induction and training programmes to help them do so. Induction and training given to Novotel staff are explained in Chapter 2.3.

Two sets of skills that are important to the successful delivery of customer service are interpersonal skills and technical skills.

Interpersonal skills

Interpersonal skills are the skills of dealing with people, including customers. Examples of such skills are the ability to be calm and diplomatic, to empathise and listen, to use appropriate language (including body language), to sell, and the ability to know when to pass a tricky or unfamiliar situation on to a colleague.

Travel and tourism customer service staff need good knowledge of the organisation, its products and services. The ability to provide accurate information is a major component of successful customer service. Not all staff in an organisation can know everything. Therefore, knowledge of where to look or which other member of staff to approach (as an internal customer) in order to resolve an external customer's information needs is crucial.

Good product knowledge helps build confidence as well as efficiency into dealings with customers. A confident and efficient member of staff will be calm and ordered in their dealings with customers.

Empathy — the ability to place oneself in the customer's position and, in the case of customer service, to communicate to the customer that their situation is understood — is an important quality. Experience in dealing with different types of customer helps build empathy.

Careful listening, appropriate demeanour, receptive body language and diplomatic language are important attributes of a successful face-to-face customer service encounter. For example, a front-of-house hotel staff member approaches an elderly woman who has arrived early in the hotel foyer to meet a friend. Would the customer like a cup of coffee in the meantime? The staff member should approach discretely and respectfully, opening the interchange with an ice-breaking smile. Standing in a relaxed but not too casual posture, close enough to engage the customer without their conversation becoming public and yet not so close as to invade the customer's personal space, helps to relax the customer and make her feel she is being looked after.

Technical skills

Technical skills are the specialised skills travel and tourism people need to do their jobs. Technical skills include the use of hardware such as computers and point-of-sale equipment and software such as online reservation systems. Technical skills also include the ability to carry out an individual travel and tourism organisation's processes correctly — for example, how a customer's complaint is to be dealt with. These skills are covered in more detail in Chapter 2.5.

Selling

Many travel and tourism organisations are commercial organisations. Sales of holidays, travel tickets, accommodation, attraction admissions and chargeable support services are vital. Customers purchase the products and services that travel and tourism organisations sell, so customer service needs to ensure that sales are made.

Good product knowledge and well-developed interpersonal skills of dealing with people build confidence in customers, which encourages them to make bookings and buy other products and services like tickets. Management and staff need to make sure that customers are aware of the range of products and services available. Promotional materials and marketing techniques are a part of this. For example, hotels usually place lists of services available in the hotel and promotional materials, such as the restaurant menu, in guest rooms. This is marketing that overlaps into customer service.

Interacting with customers to make sales often requires prompt responses. For example, if a customer telephones a direct-sell tour operator or a hotel with an availability enquiry, a speedy reply is more likely to lead to a booking. Closing the sale is an important part of selling. If a travel agency customer is trying to choose between several options for a holiday, the travel consultant needs to have the skill to judge when it is appropriate to suggest a decision. Too much pressure may deter the customer, but advice that is too vague may lead to the customer walking out of the agency without deciding, and then possibly booking elsewhere. Correctly judging the moment to bring the sale to a close is a skill gained through experience of dealing with customers.

Practical scenarios

As a travel and tourism student, you need to learn, practise and demonstrate customer service skills. In real travel and tourism workplace situations, or in imaginary scenarios, you need to develop practical skills of dealing with customers.

Role play

Role play is a valuable method of doing this. Face-to-face role plays allow you to practise oral communication skills. However, the playing of roles need not be restricted to face-to-face customer service or to telephone calls. Writing a letter or composing an e-mail for an imaginary customer in the role of a travel and tourism professional are equally valid scenarios.

A range of examples of customer service scenarios linked to case-study travel and tourism organisations from the six sectors of the industry is given below. These can be adapted to different customer types in different customer service situations from other sectors of the travel and tourism industry to provide more opportunities for practice.

Customer service scenarios

1

Scenario: at the theme park. During a routine early-morning inspection, a technical difficulty with a roller coaster ride has become evident. This is communicated by the member of staff at the ride entrance where a small queue of early visitors has formed. There are pairs of adults, a group of teenagers and a family group.

Good morning, everyone. I'm sorry to tell you that we have a technical problem with the ride and are not able to open it at the moment.

When will it open?

At the moment, I'm not able to say when it will reopen. Our engineers are working on the problem now. I can give you pass tickets so that you can enjoy the ride later today, if it's repaired, and you won't have to queue.

OK. We'll come back later.

We'll wait a while to see if it's repaired soon. It's my daughter's favourite ride and we've come early especially to go on it a few times. Is it OK to wait?

That's fine, sir. I understand. You do realise that I can't say when it will reopen at the moment. It may not be today — I don't know.

It's my favourite too, but there's a new ride just opened this year over there — I'm sure you'd like that.

OK. We understand. We'll give it 20 minutes or so and see if you know anything more. If you don't, we'll take the pass for later and maybe try the new ride out.

David du Plessis

Conclusion: the ride is not repaired 20 minutes later. The engineers are still working on it. The family group takes a pass and decides to go on another ride. After ice creams, they return to the original ride and use the pass to board it straight away. The daughter has another go later and they leave happy.

By evaluating the customer service given by the theme park ride attendant in Figure 2.30, strengths and weaknesses can be identified. As far as the strengths are concerned, the member of staff was polite and kept the customers clearly informed to the best of her ability. Her information was accurate, and she did not raise hopes by making over-optimistic forecasts as to what would happen. A compensatory offer of a pass to use the ride later without queuing was sufficient to satisfy customers without costing the theme park any revenue. Travel and tourism organisation managements do not usually encourage staff to

Figure 2.30 A face-to-face customer service scenario at a visitor attraction

make excessively generous offers to customers at the first signs of difficulty. Such offers are usually not necessary and are ultimately expensive. Empathy with the family is shown. The attendant took the trouble to have a special word with the disappointed daughter, gently suggesting an alternative without pushing it too hard. The family were allowed to continue to wait (their choice), but the fact that waiting may not make any difference was explained to them. On their later return to the ride, the pass system worked well and the customers were able to access the ride without delays.

The strengths outweigh the weaknesses, but it was not made clear what would happen if the ride could not be repaired that day. No one actually asked. The attendant hopefully knew, or at least knew whom she should contact for further advice, if the issue was raised. A voucher for free refreshments might be appropriate compensation. Free admission to the theme park would probably be considered excessively generous and would only be allowed by a senior staff member such as the duty manager.

The customers left happy. However, the theme park management does not know this because the customers were not asked. Monitoring customer satisfaction is important in ensuring that they come back and tell other people how well they were treated. Ways in which this is done by travel and tourism organisations are explained in Chapter 2.6.

Of course, the ride should not have gone wrong in the first place. However, nothing in the real world is perfect all the time. Things do go wrong, even in the best-managed travel and tourism organisation. More importantly, the maintenance engineers were addressing the technical problem at once, and health and safety considerations had taken precedence as the ride was closed immediately after routine testing showed a difficulty.

Evaluating customer service is important in developing customer service skills. Further practical scenarios in this chapter allow opportunities for you to balance their strengths and weaknesses so that you can apply them in role-play simulations or in real work placements. The scenarios presented here are intended as examples of good practice, so strengths should outweigh weaknesses. However, that does not mean there is not room for discussion of shortcomings or possible improvements, even where customer service is already good. Observing real customer service situations, perhaps in a work-shadowing situation, will provide more chances still.

2

Figure 2.31 A tour operator's telephone dialogue

David du Plessis

Figure 2.31 is part of a telephone conversation between a customer and a tour operator from whom the customer buys a holiday directly. Concentrating on the selling aspect, a strength of this exchange is that the tour operator closed the sale by taking the deposit. This has not happened by accident. The tour operator has identified a product that suits the customer's needs and clarified the scarcity of what the customer wants. The client is presented with a situation in which the property that will suit his family is available but in short supply. He books it.

3 Kim, a member of staff at a coach operator's customer service centre, has taken down a message from an answerphone (Figure 2.32). This concerns a scheduled coach service of the previous evening. She has passed the message on to a colleague. The colleague needs to investigate the customer's complaint and will inform the customer of this when he calls back. Company policy, assuming the complaint is justified, is to offer to send a £5 travel voucher as compensation.

Message from: Mr Rickerby

Time: 9 am

Date: 16 Feb

Message content: The 19.55 coach from London Heathrow to Woking did not appear. Customer waited over an hour. Ringing back later. Wants to know what happened and what we'll do about it.

Message taken by: Kim from answerphone

Figure 2.32 Kim's answerphone message transcript

4 Figure 2.33 shows the text of an e-mail exchange between a tourist and a member of staff in a tourist information office.

Figure 2.33 E-mails between a tourist and a tourist information office

To: The Tourist Information Office

Subject: Directions to the Scott Monument

I'm travelling by train to Edinburgh next week, arriving at Waverley station mid-morning. I want to get to the Scott Monument where I'm meeting a colleague. Please can you give me directions?

Many thanks.

Jo Thornton

To: Jo Thornton

Subject: RE: Directions to the Scott Monument

Thank you for your enquiry. Leave Waverley Station and cross the road to Prince Street Gardens. Walk straight on, through the gardens towards the Scott Monument, which is a tall stone structure that you will see easily.

I'm attaching a picture of the Scott Monument and a street map for your information.

I hope you find this information useful and that you enjoy your visit to Edinburgh. Please do not hesitate to contact us again if you require any further assistance.

Tourist Information Office

5 Customer service situations can also include letter writing. In the case illustrated by Figure 2.34, the reservations manager of a hotel is responding to a customer request to supply written confirmation of a booking made on the telephone.

The Coram Hotel
Coram Hill
Bishopborough

23 March

Dear Mrs Ali

Further to our telephone conversation today, I write as agreed to confirm your booking for the weekend of 20 to 22 May.

Arrival: Friday 20 May

Two sea-view rooms, one superior (one adult and one child) and one executive (two adults). Non-smoking. Breakfasts and dinners on both days.

Departure: Sunday 22 May

We very much look forward to welcoming you at The Coram Hotel on 20 May.

Yours sincerely

Nicholas Collingwood

Nicholas Collingwood
Reservations Manager

Figure 2.34
A booking confirmation letter from a hotel

> **Discussion point**
>
> What are the strengths of the customer service provided in the practical scenarios in this chapter? Are there significant weaknesses?

There are also examples of customer service scenarios in Chapters 2.2 and 2.3, including several from Novotel's Service Extraordinaire staff training programme.

Evidence of dealing with customers

Real workplace customer service situations and role-play simulations can be witnessed in various ways, as shown in Table 2.3.

Situation	Evidence
Face to face	• Witness statement: a named individual, whose job title is clearly shown, should sign any witness statement. The witness should be in a position to assess the quality of customer service given, e.g. a teacher or line manager. • Transcript of the exchange. • Evaluations: perhaps written using a writing frame. Evaluators can include peers, oneself, a teacher or a line manager. • Recording: video (DVD menus are useful ways of tracking its contents) or audio.
Telephone call	• Witness statement • Transcript • Evaluations • Recording
Answerphone message taking and response	Copies. Annotated versions pointing out strengths and weaknesses and justifying responses are more powerful.
E-mail	
Letter writing	

Table 2.3 Evidencing customer service

Support your learning

Information sources

Many travel and tourism organisations have training materials that include examples of good practice. Work shadowing is an opportunity to observe customer service in practice and to learn from that.

Skills builder

Role play customer service scenarios. Have face-to-face and oral communications witnessed and act on evaluation feedback from witnesses to improve subsequent role plays.

Activities menu

1 *Vocational scenario*
 Imagine you are the training manager of a travel and tourism organisation. Prepare training materials to illustrate good customer service practice in scenarios involving oral communication.

2 Apply the examples of customer service shown in the practical scenarios to situations in travel and tourism organisations belonging to other sectors.

3 Research and analyse customer service given in a variety of real travel and tourism organisations.

4 Evaluate the strengths and weaknesses of customer service given in a variety of travel and tourism customer service situations. Scenarios may be real or imaginary.

2.5

Technical skills for travel and tourism

Technical skills are the specialised skills travel and tourism people need to do their jobs. They include the use of hardware such as computers and point-of-sale equipment, as well as systems such as ViewData and computerised reservation systems (CRS). Other technical skills that travel and tourism staff may need are:

- skills of dealing with customers (see Chapter 2.4) face to face and using written communication, including e-mails and letters
- word processing
- payment-processing skills involving cash, cheques and debit/credit cards
- currency conversion and foreign exchange transaction handling
- telephone call handling

Case study: Travelodge

Travelodge is an accommodation provider. The organisation has over 230 **convenience hotels** in cities and alongside main roads in the UK and Ireland. Convenience hotels target the business tourist market. They are priced relatively cheaply and concentrate on providing a restricted range of good-quality services for their guests. Concentrating on core services of reception, room accommodation (Figure 2.35) and housekeeping in purpose-built, simply designed buildings allows convenience hotels to run with lower staffing levels than traditional hotels. They tend to offer a broader range of services, often including non-resident services such as functions like wedding receptions, trade fairs and business conferences.

The Travelodge reservations system is **centralised**. Travelodge employs 260 people at its reservations centre in Dudley in the West Midlands, where staff take bookings for Travelodges nationwide. Customers can also make reservations using the Travelodge website at

Figure 2.35
The Travelodge organisation focuses on core services like guest bedrooms

www.travelodge.co.uk. Operating costs are reduced by keeping the number of staff needed at each hotel relatively low while, at the same time, allowing them to concentrate on providing service to customers.

To train staff in handling telephone calls to the standard required by Travelodge's management, the organisation's human resources and training department engaged the services of an outside training provider (TTC Training), which meant that Travelodge staff were able to gain nationally recognised qualifications in call handling. Using an outside training provider was preferred by Travelodge because it enabled its management to concentrate on running the organisation's operation and marketing the brand. Well-trained internal customers provide better customer service to organisations' external customers, which is important in ensuring repeat business and in marketing the organisation. Satisfied customers are also likely to recommend the organisation to other potential customers, increasing revenue.

Other organisations sometimes prefer to make use of in-house training where employees receive training in technical skills within the organisation from more experienced colleagues, such as the hotel coach system used by Novotel. This scheme is explained in Chapter 2.3. In-house, on-the-job training in technical skills is easier to resource because there are more people available to deliver the training.

Technical skills also include the ability to carry out an individual travel and tourism organisation's processes correctly — for example, the way in which a customer's complaint is to be handled.

Travel and tourism organisations use their staff induction programmes to introduce new staff to the expected ways of carrying out their roles in the organisation they have just joined. Staff training programmes can be used to develop technical skills and to help established staff keep up to date with recent changes, such as new equipment and software.

Figure 2.36 describes the job of travel adviser at a Going Places travel agency. A travel adviser is another term for a travel consultant. Going Places is part of the My Travel group of travel and tourism companies. Enthusiasm and people skills are emphasised by My Travel in recruiting retail staff to work in travel agencies like the Going Places chain. Product knowledge is gained by learning, and experience is gained on the job and by sharing good practice with other team members in the travel agency. My Travel offers induction and ongoing training and development in technical and other customer service skills to its staff. The My Travel job application form asks what travel and tourism qualifications the applicant has, so a qualification in a technical skill could be an advantage.

TRAVEL ADVISER ✈✈✈✈

You will deliver memorable service by helping your customer find the perfect holiday. You will give them real insight into resorts so they feel like they are there before they even leave the store. You will be bringing the pictures in our brochures to life just by talking to our customers.

You will have an outgoing approach, a friendly personality and a genuine passion for travel.

You will gain product knowledge through learning and experience, and use this effectively with every customer, ensuring you meet all your sales targets.

You will contribute to the success of your store by sharing ideas and working as part of a team.

If you have customer service experience, a keen interest in travel and are looking for an exciting career with prospects, then this could be the role for you!

Source: www.mytravel.com

Figure 2.36 Job description of a travel adviser at Going Places

Discussion point ⬤

How far does a travel and tourism qualification help people to get jobs in travel and tourism organisations such as travel agencies?

ViewData

Travel consultants need to have the technical skill of using ViewData systems. Training providers such as TTC Training, which runs the Travel Training Programme, offer courses in various systems in local colleges in the UK.

ViewData is the name for systems used by travel agents to access the computerised reservation systems (CRS) of tour operators and transport principals such as airlines. Using telephone lines, the screen on the travel consultant's desk is linked via a ViewData switch to the tour operator or transport principal's host computer so that the consultant can view its data. The appearance onscreen of ViewData is similar to that of Teletext. Figure 2.37 is an example screen display where ViewData has enabled access to the tour operator Thomson's host computer (TOP).

Centrepoint Management Services Ltd/Thomson

Figure 2.37 A ViewData display

Examples of ViewData systems used in the UK travel and tourism industry are Istel and Fastrak. ViewData is a gateway. It enables travel consultants to access computerised reservation systems and advise customers instantly about the availability of package holidays advertised in brochures, about special deals that may be available and the availability of airline seats and cabins on cruise ships. Based on the data a consultant views, he/she can discuss the options with the customer and close a sale by making a booking there and then.

Travel agencies characteristically have a furniture arrangement that includes desks and seats (Figure 2.38). In this way, customers are comfortably seated while the consultant uses the firm's ViewData system to explore options. Psychologically this means that it is more difficult for the client not to accept an option discussed with the consultant — the customer is in the position of having to turn an offer down, collect their belongings and any brochures they have been given, stand up and leave the shop. If the consultant has used customer service skills to establish empathy and rapport with the customer, this is less likely still.

Traditional high-street travel agents are located close to their competitors. The organisations' management is concerned that customers do not simply go next door to book their holiday there. Once the client is seated, they hope the consultant will make a sale. ViewData access to computerised reservation systems is a valuable tool that they use to try to ensure this happens.

Figure 2.38 *Seated customers in a travel agency*

Topfoto

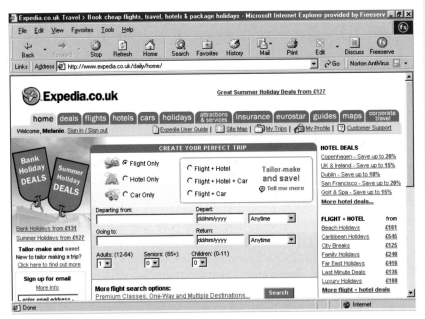

Figure 2.39 The Expedia website welcomes clients when they log on

Computerised reservation systems used by travel agencies in the UK include Galileo and Amadeus. Sabre is the name of a global CRS that was developed originally by American Airlines. Tour operators have had their own computerised reservation systems. Thomson, for example, has a system called TOP that travel agents can access via their ViewData system, allowing them to offer customers an instant Thomson alternative if their first-choice holiday is already booked. Tour operators such as Thomson do not want to lose a **potential customer**. ViewData and the CRS make it more likely that they will secure the client as an **actual customer**. Potential customers are people who have not yet booked or otherwise become part of the travel and tourism organisation's client base, whereas actual customers have made a booking. In the case of an online travel booker such as Expedia, people register as customers on the website, usually when they make their first booking. Part of the selling approach of such organisations is to welcome the customer by name each time they log onto their website (Figure 2.39).

Computerised reservation systems are interactive, which means the availability situations they describe are constantly and instantly updated. Therefore, if a travel consultant makes an airline seat booking, that seat will instantly be withdrawn from the market. This is essential for CRSs to have credibility; otherwise there would be a danger of the same product or service being sold twice by different travel consultants.

Support your learning

Information sources

Travel and tourism organisations' websites often include job descriptions and person specifications so you can assess the importance of technical skills. The TTC Training website at **www.ttctraining.co.uk** gives information about courses in acquiring technical skills for the travel and tourism industry.

Skills builder

1 ViewData is available to travel agents. Try to get a travel agency work placement, work-shadowing opportunity or visit, and ask to try it out.

2 Act as a travel agent yourself by using tour operator and transport principal websites to price and assess availability of travel options. Simulate the tour operator role by assembling a package from components available on the internet.

Activities menu

1 Outline the technical skills needed by a travel consultant.

2 *Vocational scenario*
   Imagine the tour operator Village Holidays (see Chapter 2.2) is recruiting a new member of staff to run the UK office while the partners research more properties in France. Prepare a job description that clarifies the range of technical skills needed.

3 Research and analyse the technical skills needed to succeed in any one travel and tourism career.

4 Evaluate the extent to which technical skills needed for success in any one travel and tourism job role may be acquired during training after appointment.

2.6

Quality of customer service

Evaluating customer service in travel and tourism

Travel and tourism managers undertake evaluations of the customer service provided by their organisation. This is true for travel and tourism organisations in all six sectors of the industry. Various techniques are used.

Benchmarks and targets

A **benchmark** is a set standard against which performance is measured. Travel and tourism organisation managements may set standards to use as measures of the quality of their customer service. For example, the percentage of very satisfied customers may be used to set the benchmark. If 78% were very satisfied in Year 1, that may be regarded as the benchmark against which to measure the next year's quality of customer service. If it exceeds 78%, that will be a success; if it is lower than 78%, there will be an issue to resolve.

Other benchmarks that may be used to monitor customer service performance in travel and tourism organisations are based on criteria such as the length of time people wait before being served, the number of complaints received and the percentage of people who would recommend the organisation to a friend or who return with repeat business.

Benchmarking can be used by travel and tourism organisations belonging to each sector of the industry. A tourist information office, for example, may use waiting times (Figure 2.40). A benchmark may be a wait of 3 minutes before a staff member serves a customer. Transport and accommodation providers may find percentage data of satisfied customers, complaints received and repeat business useful benchmark-setting material.

Topfoto

Figure 2.40 *Tourist information offices may use waiting times as a benchmark*

Targets are goals to which the management of a travel and tourism organisation may aspire. They may set customer service quality targets. Although the target figure and the benchmark figure may be the same, this is not always the case. There is a difference in meaning. Taking the example of 78% customer satisfaction in Year 1 again, the management may decide that 80% could be achieved realistically in Year 2. That is the target success figure. The benchmark of 78% is what the level of success is measured against.

Questionnaires

The results of customer questionnaires can be analysed for levels of satisfaction that can then be used as benchmarks to judge future success. For example, Figure 2.41 shows part of the guest room questionnaire completed by guests of Novotel in the UK. The section headed 'Are you satisfied?' includes six criteria. For the final question, 'Would you be happy to stay at this hotel again?', the management can add up customer responses and express them as percentages across all Accor Hotels in the UK, all Novotels in the UK (Novotel is one of Accor's **brands**) and for each Novotel in the UK that year. The following year's performance at any one hotel can then be judged against:

- its own performance the previous year
- the average performances of Novotels and Accor Hotels in general across the UK

ABOUT YOU? - QUI ÊTES-VOUS ?

Location of Novotel at which you stayed: _____
Vous avez séjourné à l'hôtel de: _____

Room N°: _____ from _____ to _____
Dans la chambre N°: _____ du _____ au _____

Title: _____
Titre: _____

Your name: _____ Initial: _____
Votre nom: _____

Your address: _____
Votre adresse: _____

Postcode: _____

Purpose of your stay: Business ☐ Personal ☐ In a tour group ☐
Les raisons de votre séjour, à titre: Professional ☐ Privé ☐ En groupe touristique ☐

Are you an Accor Hotels Favorite Guest Cardholder? Yes ☐ No ☐
Êtes-vous porteur de la carte Accor Hotels Favorite Guest ? Oui ☐ Non ☐

Do you stay more than 10 nights per year in a Novotel hotel? Yes ☐ No ☐
Séjournez-vous plus de 10 nuits par an, dans le réseau Novotel ? Oui ☐ Non ☐

ARE YOU SATISFIED? - ÊTES-VOUS SATISFAIT ?

Your accommodation Yes ☐ No ☐
De votre hébergement Oui ☐ Non ☐

Food and Beverage Yes ☐ No ☐
De la restauration Oui ☐ Non ☐

Breakfasts Yes ☐ No ☐
Du petit déjeuner Oui ☐ Non ☐

Service in general Yes ☐ No ☐
Du service en général Oui ☐ Non ☐

Your stay at this hotel Yes ☐ No ☐
De votre séjour dans cet hôtel Oui ☐ Non ☐

Would you be happy to stay at this hotel again? Yes ☐ No ☐
Reviendrez-vous volontiers dans cet hôtel? Oui ☐ Non ☐

Figure 2.41
An extract from the Novotel guest room customer service questionnaire

The data generated can also be used to set targets, e.g. the hotel must at least perform as well as the national average for other hotels in the group.

Mystery shoppers

Mystery shoppers act as members of the public (external customers). In reality, however, they are not. They may be travel and tourism professionals posing as ordinary members of the public to test the quality of customer service provided. Examples of travel and tourism facilities where customer service can be tested in this way include

high-street and out-of-town travel agencies (which are essentially shops), direct-sell tour operators (by telephone), hotel reception and catering facilities, transport provider and visitor attraction ticket and booking offices, tourist information offices and external customer support services.

Mystery shoppers may use checklists of criteria, e.g. the length of time they waited, the greeting they received, the appearance and manner of the staff members, the quality of overall service and the extent to which they were satisfied with the outcome. To assist in comparing standards between organisations, or from one time to another, scoring systems can be used, giving 1 for a very weak and 5 for a very strong aspect of service, for example.

Mystery shoppers would obviously not be mysterious if they used checklists mounted on clipboards while in the facility under test. They are much more likely to complete any information immediately following their exit, assuming that they are testing face-to-face customer service. Telephone customer service lends itself to mystery shopper testing.

The key advantage of the mystery shopper approach is that the staff member providing the customer service is unaware that an observation is taking place and so is more likely to provide the usual level of customer service — not a better one for the benefit of the tester. Travel and tourism organisations also use mystery shoppers to investigate the customer service quality provided by competitors including travel agencies, hotels or airlines. Such data can be valuable in setting benchmarks and targets.

Observation

Travel and tourism managers observe staff delivering customer service and provide feedback on strengths and weaknesses of their delivery to help their staff to develop professionally as individuals and to benefit the organisation as a whole. This is part of ongoing staff training. Training observations can also involve staff observing colleagues and, often as part of induction, watching more experienced colleagues deliver customer service. For a travel and tourism student, observation as part of a work-shadowing opportunity can be a valuable learning experience.

Senior staff can keep an eye on customer service delivery in a less formal way too, by observing a colleague engaged in discussion with a customer in a travel agency, walking the floor in a hotel and observing customer service in situations such as reception and in the bar and restaurant (Figure 2.42).

Informal feedback

Customer service staff and travel and tourism managers can pick up customer feedback just by dealing with people and watching and listening to them. In hotels, staff in the lobby area, for example, will be aware of customer perceptions of the service being provided simply by overhearing comments. Such an informal collection of customer feelings is not organised or, by any means, a statistical sample, but travel and tourism managers would not wish to ignore it. Staff training can be used to educate staff in the importance of listening to what customers have to say and feeding this back to managers.

On a train, for example, staff members move up and down the passenger compartments of the carriages to serve refreshments and to check tickets. They pick up customer feeling as they do so. Train company managers are naturally interested in what they have heard. Knowing, in particular, what customers feel less than happy with is vital in managing change so that customers are satisfied. Satisfied customers will return and tell other people about the advantages of using the train service the company provides. Customers provide the money that keeps the organisation in business.

Figure 2.42 Hotel management can observe customer service in the bar and restaurant

©Jupiterimages/www.comstock.com

Focus groups

A focus group session is a meeting of a small number of people concentrating on one topic or focus. The manager of a travel and tourism organisation that provides services for a range of organisations may wish to review the standard of customer service the organisations are receiving and know what improvements they would suggest. One method of doing this is to invite some of the organisations to send a representative to a focus group meeting. By talking to each other, ideas may be shared in addition to those that could have been obtained by completing questionnaires in isolation.

Suggestion boxes

Suggestion boxes are a cheap and simple way to collect customer views, usually as they leave. A visitor attraction may place a box next to the exit door; a hotel may have a 'drop' at reception for guests to deposit keys and comment cards as part of an express check-out facility.

A real example of an organisation monitoring the quality of its customer service is given below.

Case study: Novotel hotels

As part of their Service Extraordinaire initiative (see Chapter 2.3), Novotel hotels has adopted tools that include:

- the Qualisurvey
- the floor-walk
- the image check-up

The Qualisurvey

Early each day, face-to-face interviews are held with hotel guests. During the interview, the manager records the customer's comments using the form shown in Figure 2.43. At the Novotel York, five or six external customers are interviewed daily. A senior staff member, such as the general manager, approaches guests in the hotel lobby and asks them to take part — most are happy to do so. They sit down together and talk through the guests' experiences at the hotel.

Staff undertaking this task are senior personnel who have received training in dealing with customer complaints. It is important that the guest feels able to share anything that has not lived up to their expectations without the staff member seeming offended by this. The general manager is keen to discover any downsides to customer service that guests have received. From a travel and tourism management perspective, it is much better that even minor dissatisfactions are known and can be acted upon than that the customer expresses dissatisfaction to others (potential customers) after they have left. If the organisation is not aware of any dissatisfaction, it cannot be addressed and business may be damaged. Feedback is discussed at each morning's management meeting — see below.

Can I take a few minutes of your time to ask you some questions about the service during your stay with us?

Business or Leisure:

Room No:

Date:

Completed by:

	agree strongly	agree	disagree	disagree strongly

Would you describe your stay here as 'hassle-free'?

If not, where do you feel there are hassles that you would like to see us take out of your way?

	agree strongly	agree	disagree	disagree strongly

Did you find staff went out of their way to help you?

If not, what areas of our service could we improve, and were there any specific cases where you would have liked help of this kind?

	agree strongly	agree	disagree	disagree strongly

Did you find the hotel as a whole a relaxed and comfortable place to stay?

If not, what aspects did you not find relaxing or comfortable?

	agree strongly	agree	disagree	disagree strongly

During your stay, did you find any examples of a 'human touch' in our service?

If so, please let us know where and who, and if there are any areas of the hotel where you feel we should work on this more.

Figure 2.43 *The Qualisurvey form*

The floor-walk

A senior member of staff or the hotel coach walks round the hotel every day. The hotel coach is a member of Novotel staff who has training and staff development responsibilities. The role of the hotel coach is explained in more detail in Chapter 2.3. The floor-walker checks each of the hotel's departments; in the case of the Novotel York, these are front of house, food and beverage, housekeeping and maintenance. Customer service delivery and staff grooming standards are observed and reported to each head of department.

The image check-up

In each hotel, the management does random observations of telephone answering and e-mail- and fax-sending to monitor the standard of

communications to customers outside the hotel. The Qualisurvey and the floor-walk measure customer service inside the hotel.

Other quality measures

The three Service Extraordinaire tools described above are not the only customer service quality measures used at Novotels in the UK. One other is the guest room customer comment card. Figure 2.41 shows the main section of one of these. Every time a room is prepared for new customers, one of these cards is left there. As well as the extract shown in Figure 2.41, there is another section for the customer to write comments and suggestions. This has over 30 lines of space on which they can write. The customer can hand in their comments when they check out or post them later. The Accor Hotels parent company freepost address is pre-printed on the envelope.

Daily management meetings

At the Novotel York, daily management meetings are held at 10.30 a.m. each day. They include the four department heads as well as the general manager. Any issues raised by the quality survey measures, including the floor-walk and the image check-up, are dealt with immediately. Nevertheless, changes can take time to work through even if action is decided upon at once.

One example at the Novotel York concerned a housekeeping department issue. The way that beds were made had drawn the same negative comment from three guests. They did not like the duvets being tightly tucked around the beds, preferring them loose. The housekeeping staff were used to the old system and needed to be retrained in the new method. As several customers had commented on a particular issue, changes had to be made.

Discussion point ⬤

What views may staff and customers have about Novotel's methods of monitoring customer service quality?

Practical scenarios

As a travel and tourism student, you can be practically involved, researching and evaluating the quality of customer service provided by a travel and tourism organisation or by a sector of the travel and tourism provision in an area, such as the travel agencies in your local town.

Some of the techniques explained in this chapter are readily applicable to such a practical scenario. Mystery shoppers, questionnaires, observation and focus groups are methods of collecting data for evaluation that you can use. Your approach may be quantitative (using scoring systems on a mystery shopper checklist, for example) or qualitative.

Quantitative data are useful in allowing you to combine data from several observations or to compare the customer service quality of several travel and tourism organisations.

You can make the mystery shopper method a group or class activity. Divide the town's travel agencies between you and agree on some common testing criteria. These might include:

- how long you waited to get served
- how polite the staff were
- whether you were offered a brochure to take away

You should agree a system of scoring these qualities.

Customers of travel and tourism organisations are all around you. Many people in your school or college will, for example, have been customers of your nearest airport. You can survey their opinion of aspects of customer service they received using a questionnaire or put together a focus group to discuss their views.

Support your learning

Information sources

Travel and tourism organisations often have customer comment cards or questionnaires that they use to collect feedback from their own customers.

Skills builder

Work on the practical scenarios by developing customer questionnaires or mystery shopper checklists.

Activities menu

1 a Explain the difference between benchmarks and targets.
   b Explain how other customer service quality monitoring techniques can help set benchmarks and targets.

2 Investigate the quality of customer service provided by local travel agencies using the mystery shopper approach. Design a checklist to enable you to do this.

3 *Vocational scenario*
   Imagine a travel and tourism organisation has been taken over. The management of the parent company wants to learn more about the travel and tourism organisation's customer service quality. As a customer service manager, you have been asked to undertake the following tasks:
   a Research and analyse the customer service quality monitoring techniques used by the travel and tourism organisation.
   b Evaluate the feasibility of using different methods in the future.

3

Travel destinations

Starter:
where tourists go

People travel mostly for leisure (e.g. on holiday), for business reasons or to visit friends and relatives (VFR). The places tourists visit are tourist destinations. Destinations for business tourists are predominantly cities, often capital cities, and certainly places where industry and commerce are concentrated. In capital cities like London, the transport and accommodation provider sectors of the travel and tourism industry cater for business (as well as leisure) tourists, who use the city as a central place to meet colleagues from around the UK and beyond.

Types of destination

Leisure tourist destinations include cities too. London is a major UK destination. Figure 3.1 shows the UK towns most visited by overseas visitors (excluding London) in 2003. London alone had 11.7 million overnight stays by inbound tourists that year — more than 13 times as many as Edinburgh, the second most-visited city by overseas residents.

Many cities are holiday destinations. World cities much visited by leisure tourists from the UK include New York, Paris, Barcelona, Rome, Amsterdam, Prague, Cape Town and Bangkok. The locations of these cities are shown on Figures 3.2 and 3.3.

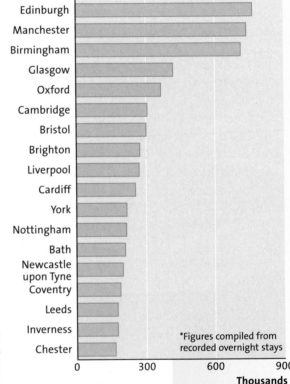

*Figures compiled from recorded overnight stays

Figure 3.1 *The top UK towns visited (excluding London) by number of overseas tourists, 2003**

Discussion point

Over half of all inbound tourist visits to the UK include at least one night spent in London. Why should this be so?

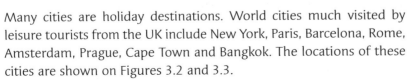

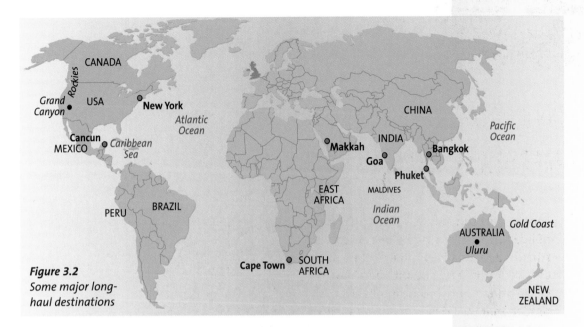

Figure 3.2
Some major long-haul destinations

Types of destination other than cities include:

■ Coastal areas, including seaside resorts — for example, Cancun, Palma, Mallorca, Cannes, the Greek Islands, Goa, the Maldives, Phuket and Australia's Gold Coast. Not all coastal areas that are destinations for leisure tourists are resorts — for example, Australia's Great Barrier Reef.

■ Countryside regions such as mountains, lakes and forests. Winter sports resorts in mountainous areas such as the Rockies and the Alps become centres for climbers, walkers and tourists wanting to see spectacular scenery in the summer months. Countryside destinations include the National Parks of western USA and Canada (including spectacular sights such as the Grand Canyon), and the UK (including the Lake District). Uluru (Ayers Rock) in Australia, the safari destinations of Africa and the Black Forest in Germany are also countryside destinations.

■ Historical and cultural destinations, including regions like the Peruvian Andes, where Inca ruins like Machu Picchu are a major draw.

■ Religious centres such as Rome and Makkah.

■ Purpose-built resorts such as Disneyland Paris and Sun City in South Africa.

Classifying holiday destinations is, like all classification systems, not entirely straightforward. Some destinations clearly belong to more

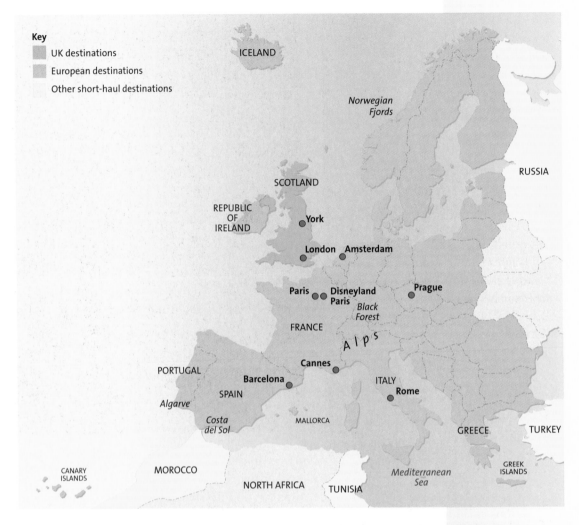

Key
- UK destinations
- European destinations
- Other short-haul destinations

ICELAND

Norwegian Fjords

RUSSIA

SCOTLAND

REPUBLIC OF IRELAND

York

London Amsterdam

Paris Disneyland Paris Prague

Black Forest

FRANCE

Alps

Cannes

PORTUGAL

Barcelona ITALY Rome

SPAIN

Algarve

Costa del Sol MALLORCA

GREECE TURKEY

CANARY ISLANDS MOROCCO

NORTH AFRICA TUNISIA

Mediterranean Sea GREEK ISLANDS

than one classification. For example, Rome is a major city tourist destination, much visited for historical and cultural reasons (Figure 3.4) as well as religious ones. However, it is useful to understand the range of tourist destinations that UK leisure travellers visit.

Figure 3.3 *Some major short-haul destinations*

Short-haul and long-haul destinations

Travel destinations visited by UK tourists are domestic if they are within the UK, short-haul if they are in Europe and in North Africa (for example, Morocco, Tunisia and Egypt), or in near Asia (examples include the Israeli Red Sea coast and most of Turkey), and long-haul if they are beyond that. Figures 3.2 and 3.3 show some major short-haul and long-haul travel destinations.

UK tourists travelling abroad are outbound from the UK. Inbound tourists to the UK are people visiting from abroad. Figure 1.2 (see the Starter in Unit 1) shows the top ten countries from which inbound tourists came to visit the UK in 2003.

Scale

The scale of tourist destinations varies. At the smallest end of the range are single settlements such as resorts, which are usually towns or cities. UK examples are Brighton, Harrogate and Edinburgh. Villages can also be leisure tourist destinations, e.g. Grasmere in the Lake District or Bourton-on-the-Water in the Cotswolds.

On a larger scale, whole areas, regions or countries can be tourist destinations, e.g. in the UK, the Antrim Coast, Snowdonia and Scotland are tourist destinations at a regional and national

Figure 3.4 *The Colosseum — Rome is a popular tourist destination for historical and cultural reasons*

Topfoto

scale. Outside the UK, the French Riviera, the Costa del Sol and Mauritius are also tourist destinations. Much larger countries such as Australia and the USA can be referred to as tourist destinations, although in reality many tourists spend much or all of their stay in a part, or several parts, of such large countries so their actual destinations are on a smaller scale.

For study purposes, resorts, cities, defined regions (such as the Algarve or the Norwegian Fjords) or small countries (e.g. islands such as Barbados) are a manageable scale of destination.

Itinerant tourism

Tourists may arrive at a particular destination and stay there, perhaps with a few excursions, for the duration of their holiday. Such single-centre holidays are often resort-based main holidays (e.g. 2 weeks in Bodrum, Turkey) or city-break short stays (e.g. a long weekend in Budapest, Hungary).

Itinerant tourists do not do this. They move around during their holiday, staying at several settlement destinations (resorts, villages or towns) within a larger destination area. A sightseeing tour of Australia, a cruise around the Greek Islands or a backpacking trip through Southeast Asia are examples of itinerant tourism. Independent travellers are often itinerant tourists. Tourists booking flight-only to an American **gateway** such as Miami and hiring a car to drive along the Gulf of Mexico coast to New Orleans, staying in roadside motels en route, are an example. A gateway is a point of entry into a country. Gateway airports are those that accept international flights bringing incoming tourists. Other gateway points of entry to a country include ports and land frontier crossings (both road and rail).

An example of a package holiday tour that is also itinerant tourism is shown in Figure 3.5.

Figure 3.5 *An example of an itinerant tour route in Italy*

8 Days
Italian Treasures

Itinerary — coach tour

Day 1	Flight from UK to Venice	*Day 5*	Rome
Day 2	Venice to Florence	*Day 6*	Rome to Assisi to Venice
Day 3	Florence	*Day 7*	Venice
Day 4	Florence to Rome	*Day 8*	Flight from Venice to the UK

Tourist-generating and tourist-receiving areas

Tourist-generating areas are regions where tourists normally live and work and from which they travel for business or leisure purposes, or to visit friends and relatives (VFR). **Tourist-receiving areas** are regions which people visit for business or leisure purposes or to visit friends and relatives. It is possible for an area to be both a tourist-generating and a tourist-receiving area. One such example is London. Londoners travel throughout the UK and the world for leisure and business tourism and to visit friends and relatives. At the same time, the 11.7 million nights spent in London in 2003 by overseas tourists alone brought £5.9 billion of spending to the city — a major economic benefit.

Traditionally, densely populated urban areas in industrialised countries were tourist-generating areas. In the early development of mass travel and tourism following the Industrial Revolution (see Chapter 1.3), many tourists travelled from the polluted cities to seaside resorts such as Blackpool, Scarborough and Brighton in the UK, and Coney Island near New York in the USA. Countryside destinations such as the English Lake District (Figure 3.6) and the Peak District also became tourist-receiving areas.

Figure 3.6 *Keswick town centre: the English Lake District became a tourist-receiving area following the Industrial Revolution*

As travel and tourism further afield developed in the twentieth century, with higher disposable incomes, paid holidays, the introduction of package holidays and the development of jet aircraft, Florida in the USA and Mediterranean resorts in Europe became popular tourist-receiving areas. In the case of Florida, US tourists travelling south for the warmer weather first fuelled this growth. By the late twentieth century, Florida had become a long-haul tourist-receiving area for tourists from other parts of the world, including from the UK.

The growth of mass tourism to Mediterranean Europe created a north–south divide, with colder, northern European industrial and

Topfoto

urban regions being tourist-generating areas and warmer, southern European seasides being tourist-receiving areas. The expansion of long-haul tourism changed this pattern, at least to some extent, making the more economically developed countries (MEDCs) tourist-generating areas and the less economically developed countries (LEDCs) tourist-receiving areas. However, the real picture is more complicated, with tourists flowing in both directions.

Discussion point

To what extent is it true that the industrial North is made up of tourist-generating areas and the warmer South of tourist-receiving areas?

Support your learning

Information sources

1 Tour operator brochures and websites, travel guidebooks and travel atlases are sources of information about travel destinations.

2 Up-to-date sources of statistical information include the National Statistics website at **www.statistics.gov.uk** and the accompanying *Travel Trends* report that can be downloaded from it.

Skills builder

Graph and analyse statistics accessed from up-to-date sources.

Activities menu

1 Compile a table giving travel destinations. Classify your destinations by type and by whether, for UK tourists, they are domestic, European, other short-haul or long-haul destinations.

2 *Vocational scenario*
Imagine a short-haul tour operator has decided to introduce a limited number of long-haul destinations into its programme. You are employed as a consultant to propose these destinations.
 a Produce a map showing the locations of your chosen destinations. Briefly justify the choices you make.
 b Research and analyse the travel options open to the tour operator to transport its customers from the UK to one of your chosen destinations.
 c Evaluate the appeal of one of your chosen destinations to any one customer type.

3.1

Destination Europe

Types of European destination

Figure 3.3 in the Topic 3 Starter shows the location of some major European destinations outside the UK.

Cities

Continental European cities are popular destinations for UK leisure and business tourists. Some, such as Paris and Amsterdam, clearly cater for both. However, cities such as Frankfurt, an important industrial and commercial centre in Germany, have more appeal for UK business tourists than for holidaymakers. Other European cities that attract British tourists include Dublin, Madrid, Barcelona, Geneva, Milan, Berlin, Vienna, Prague and Budapest. Because of the European Union (EU), Brussels (seat of the European Commission) and Strasbourg (home of the European parliament) are major business tourism destinations.

Since the 1990s, two key changes have been the growth of budget airlines such as easyJet and Ryanair and the increasing integration of eastern and western Europe following the collapse of communism in the East. Cities such as Prague and Budapest have attracted more UK tourists as a result of these changes. Budget airlines have also opened up leisure travel to a wider variety of European cities. Cities such as Reykjavik in Iceland and Bologna in Italy have developed as UK tourist destinations following their inclusion in budget airline flight networks.

Historical and cultural destinations

Historical and cultural destinations are often cities. Part of the appeal of many European destinations for UK tourists is their historical legacy — historic buildings and important art galleries such as Notre Dame Cathedral and the Louvre art gallery in Paris are attractions of this type. Venice is a major leisure tourist destination largely because of its historic core including its trademark canals, St Mark's Square and the famous Rialto Bridge (Figure 3.7). Religious centres such as Rome

Figure 3.7 *The Rialto Bridge in Venice*   **Figure 3.8** *The Palais des Papes, Avignon*

attract tourists for that reason, as well as for its general city appeal and historic monuments such as the Colosseum (Figure 3.4). Avignon in southern France was the home of the popes in the fourteenth century and its Palais des Papes (Palace of the Popes) attracts tourists for both religious and historic reasons (Figure 3.8). The annual Avignon Festival is an example of how an arts event can be a major part of a city's tourist appeal.

Coastal areas

Coastal destinations, including seaside resorts visited by package holidaymakers, stretch from the Algarve in Portugal along the northern shores of the Mediterranean Sea via the Costas of Spain and Rivieras of France and Italy east to Greece and the Greek Islands (Figure 3.9). Other Mediterranean islands and island groups important for European seaside tourism are also shown in Figure 3.9 and include Spain's Balearic Islands, of which the largest is Mallorca. Although the Canary Islands lie off the coast of Africa, as they are Spanish they can be regarded as a European destination. The resorts of Turkey's Mediterranean coast (Marmaris, for example) are actually in Asia.

Not all tourists visiting the Mediterranean resorts of Europe are package holidaymakers. There are also independent travellers and business tourists. Some coastal destinations are not resorts. These tend to be quieter, often protected parts of the coast, marketed by tour

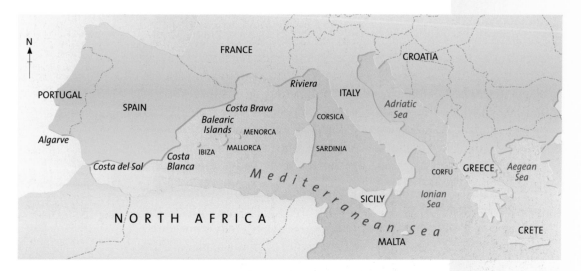

Figure 3.9 *Coastal destinations on the northern shores of the Mediterranean*

operators and their local tourist authorities as 'unspoilt'. Leaving the Mediterranean coast behind, the French Camargue on the delta of the River Rhône is one such example (Figure 3.10); the Ring of Kerry in the Irish Republic is another.

Other European destinations away from the Mediterranean that appeal strongly to tourists from the UK are found along the coasts of western and northern France, especially in Brittany and the Vendée. La Rochelle on France's Atlantic coast is a major centre whose appeal has grown even stronger as a budget airline destination. The coastlands of northern Europe, with the notable exception of the Norwegian Fjords, have tended to be less of a draw for UK tourists, although there has been some growth recently of tourism to the Baltic as republics such as Latvia and Estonia have become members of the EU.

Figure 3.10
The unspoilt Camargue on the delta of the River Rhône

Countryside regions

European countryside areas, such as mountains, lakes and forests, are popular destinations for UK tourists. Winter sports resorts in mountainous areas such as the Alps have continued to grow in popularity as skiing and snowboarding have become affordable for more British people, many of whom can ski (often the result of skiing holidays at school). Budget airlines flying to places such as Geneva have also been a major factor. These destinations become centres for climbers, walkers and tourists wanting to see spectacular scenery in the summer months.

The Austrian Tyrol, the Black Forest in Germany and the Italian Lakes are well-established inland destinations for UK leisure tourists. The package coach tour market has been a particularly well-represented sector of the UK travel and tourism industry in such places. The opening up of eastern Europe since the 1990s has led to increased UK tourist flows to destinations such as the Polish Tatra Mountains and Czech Moravian Highlands.

Coastal destinations often have nearby inland countryside regions. The inland parts of islands such as Mallorca, Ibiza, Cyprus and Crete are comparatively quiet rural backwaters, especially when compared to the bustling resorts of their shorelines. Excursions from coastal towns have sometimes created honeypot sites with their associated impacts of large tourism flows. For example, the Samaria Gorge in Crete has become a magnet for holidaymakers keen to walk its spectacular length (Figure 3.11).

Purpose-built resorts

Purpose-built resorts include destinations such as Disneyland Paris and the Center Parcs resorts. Disneyland Paris is much more than a visitor attraction. In addition to the two theme parks (the Magic Kingdom and Walt Disney Studios), it comprises the Disney Village restaurant, bar and entertainment complex; extensive grounds including golf courses; and a variety of accommodation on site. Disneyland Paris has its own transport facilities including a railway station to which Eurostar trains from the UK run, as well

Figure 3.11 The *Samaria Gorge, Crete*

Corel

as frequent French Railways services. This complexity of provision, arguably involving all sectors of the travel and tourism industry, means that it is a resort in its own right.

Types of tourist

The appeal of any destination varies according to the type of tourist concerned. Part of the skill of a travel consultant in a travel agency is to evaluate the appeal of destinations to assess those that their customer might prefer — and those they might not. The club-life of San Antonio, Ibiza, for example, is more likely appeal to some tourist types (such as parties of young, single people) than to others.

Types of tourist to consider include those listed below. Within each category are subgroups for whom the appeal of a destination may be slightly different:

- **Families**, including those with younger or older, perhaps teenage, children. The appeal of the same destination for different family members may be different and the whole family unit may be more satisfied by visiting a destination with more varied attractions.
- **Younger adults** — as single people (often in a group) or as couples, they may find different aspects of any one destination appealing.
- **Senior citizens** — the recently retired are likely to have different demands, possibly for a more active stay, from those of the elderly.
- **Special-needs customers**, including those with mobility issues, but also covering any particular needs customers may have such as dietary requirements.
- **Special-interest customers** for whom a destination may have specialist appeal. For example, a destination may offer possibilities for a walking holiday, the opportunity to view particular works of art, cater for a love of a certain style of music or satisfy a desire to learn to cook or dance in local style. Special-interest customers include those whose wish to visit a destination is motivated by a particular event like a sports fixture or pop or rock concert.

Group size

Parties made up of several people may have different demands of a destination from those of its individual members when travelling on their own or with a partner. For example, a middle-aged woman visiting a city destination like Dublin with friends from work will be likely to access different aspects of the city's appeal from those that she would on a couple-based short break with her partner.

Factors in increased popularity

Factors in the expansion of UK tourism abroad with the growth of mass tourism in the second half of the twentieth century are discussed in Chapter 1.3.

Since the 1990s, factors in the increased popularity of European destinations have been:

- **Increased consumer sophistication**: greater experience of travel, including independent travel, has created an appetite in the UK mass tourism market for more destinations. This has noticeably been the case in the city break market, where the 2005 Thomas Cook Signature Cities and Short Breaks brochure listed 40 city destinations in Europe alone, covering an A–Z range from Amsterdam to Zurich. This changed demand factor has been matched by changed factors in the supply of travel and tourism products and services for the industry.

- **Product development**: products have been developed and successfully marketed to meet the changing pattern of demand. City break packages offered by tour operators have mushroomed. In tourist-receiving areas, destination management has updated the product on offer (for example, the opening at Disneyland Paris of a second theme park, Walt Disney Studios). Promotion has also been influential. For example, the Spanish advertising campaign 'the Other Spain' has successfully showcased parts of Spain other than the mass tourist resorts of the Costas and the Balearic Islands, developing tourist destinations in inland Spain.

- **Increased online access**: internet-booking facilities accessible from tourists' home computers have made it easier for customers to surf the websites of prospective destinations and transport and accommodation providers and to make independent arrangements to visit different destinations. Allied with the growth of customer confidence that increasing travel experience has brought, previously less-visited destinations, such as Prague and Budapest in eastern Europe, have seen rising UK visitor numbers.

- **Accessibility and cost**: the rise of budget airlines and opening of the Channel Tunnel have made it easier to reach some destinations and to do so at reduced cost. The city of Lille, for example, is easily accessible by Eurostar trains operating through the Channel Tunnel from London.

- **Political factors**: the easing of tourist access to eastern Europe following the end of the Cold War has helped the development of

UK outbound tourism to destinations in countries such as the Czech Republic, Bulgaria and Poland. In addition, the expansion of the EU to include eastern-bloc countries such as the Baltic Republics has encouraged tourism flow from the UK to destinations in Estonia and Lithuania.

Case study: Port de Pollença

Location

Port de Pollença (Figure 3.12) is a Mediterranean seaside resort on the north coast of Mallorca (Majorca).

Figure 3.13 shows the location of Port de Pollença in northwest Mallorca. Mallorca is the largest of Spain's Balearic Islands. Port de Pollença is 40 km from the island's main city and international gateway, Palma.

Just inland of Port de Pollença, 6 km away as the crow flies, is the market town of Pollença. Historically, the coastline of Mallorca was frequently attacked by pirates, so people settled several kilometres inland for defensive protection rather than on the coast. The sheltered bay (the Badia de Pollença) allowed a harbour to develop at Port de Pollença. The Badia de Pollença makes it safe for today's tourists to swim.

Figure 3.12 Port de Pollença, Mallorca

Geoff Williamson/Iberimage

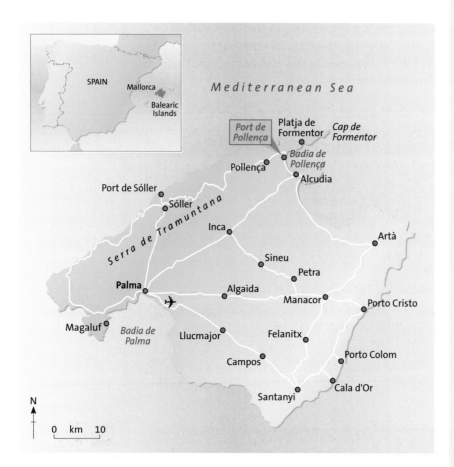

Figure 3.13
Location of Port
de Pollença in
northwest Mallorca

Landscape

Port de Pollença lies to the east of the Serra de Tramuntana mountains that form Mallorca's western shore. The village lies on the shore of a sheltered semicircular bay, the Badia de Pollença, in the shadow of the Cap de Formentor peninsula, which is the northeastern-most projection of the Serra de Tramuntana mountains. The bay has one of the few sandy beaches on Mallorca's north coast at Port de Pollença, which has been artificially extended. The landscape south of the Badia de Pollença is much gentler than its shield of the mountainous peninsula to the north, and the resort itself is generally flat. The flatlands behind the resort allow easy, scenic cycling for those tourists who wish to take advantage of the opportunity.

The 3 km-wide neck of the Cap de Formentor is traversed by a footpath allowing a hike through the Vall de Becquer to the cove of Cala Becquer beyond. This path allows tourists to appreciate the wild flowers, native shrubs and birdlife of the area, in contrast to the resort itself which, although not the noisiest, is busier in the summer months with tourists from northern Europe and more local visitors from Palma.

Climate

Figure 3.14 is a temperature graph for Palma. Table 3.1 records the average sunshine hours per day and average number of days with rain per month. From the data it can be seen that July and August are the hottest while spring and autumn remain warm and have temperatures more favourable for a sightseeing holiday. Winters are still warm enough to allow tourists to sit outside cafés in shirtsleeves in January. Hot, dry summers and mild, wet winters are characteristic of Mediterranean climates with levels of rainfall tending to be higher in the western Mediterranean basin than in the east. Mallorca is towards the wetter end.

Winter rain is, however, a climatic feature and storms can lash Mallorca's rocky western coast, driven by the prevailing westerly winds. The Serra de Tramuntana mountains act as a relief barrier to shelter much of the island from the worst effects of such storms. Port de Pollença is in the sheltered side at the foot of the eastern slopes at the northern end of these mountains and so is particularly well protected from the wind.

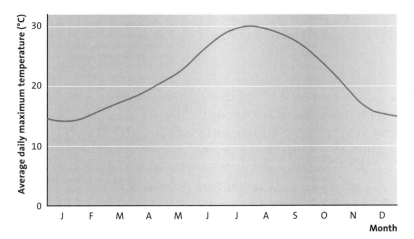

Figure 3.14
Average daily temperatures, Palma

Month	J	F	M	A	M	J	J	A	S	O	N	D
Average hours of sunshine per day	5	6	6	7	9	10	11	11	8	6	5	4
Average number of days with rain	8	6	8	6	5	3	1	3	5	9	8	9

Table 3.1 Average hours of sunshine per day and days with rain, Palma

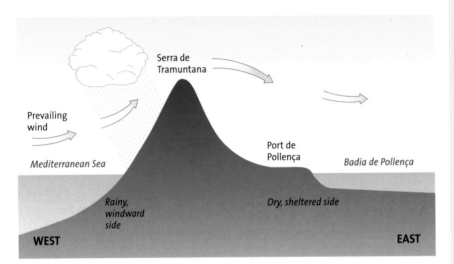

Figure 3.15
The rain-shadow effect on Port de Pollença

The situation of Port de Pollença means it benefits from the **micro-climatic** sheltering and **rain-shadow** effects of the Serra de Tramuntana mountains. The microclimate of a resort is its own local climate, which may be slightly different to the typical climate of its broader region. In this case, Port de Pollença's microclimate is relatively calm and dry in the winter months compared to the general pattern in the rest of the island. A rain shadow is a relatively dry area on the sheltered side of a relief barrier such as a mountain chain. Figure 3.15 shows Port de Pollença's rain-shadow effect.

Tourist appeal

The appeal of a destination is made up of various elements. These include:

- location and accessibility (including both ease and cost of access)
- climate and landscape
- natural and built attractions
- events
- food, drink and entertainment
- accommodation

Natural and built attractions

As Figure 3.16 shows, there are actually two attractive sandy beaches in Port de Pollença itself, with the additional Platja de Formentor a half-hour boat taxi ride away. The marina separates the Albercutx and Pollença beaches. Albercutx is the beach that runs from the marina north in front of the Pine Walk, which is a pine-shaded extension to the promenade (Figure 3.17). Albercutx beach is sometimes also known as Voramar beach. The wide sandy beach south of the marina is Pollença beach.

The beaches of Port de Pollença appeal strongly to families. There is plentiful sand, which shelves gently in to the calm bay so that the sea is calm and safe for young children to play in and for older ones to swim in. Parents can sit and relax in the seafront cafés and restaurants while their children play safely in the sand opposite.

The attractive curve of the beaches with the Pine Walk to the north and the backdrop of the mountainous Cap de Formentor make Port de Pollença also appeal to other groups including couples and senior citizens. As all the sea front from the marina to a little beyond the Pine Walk is pedestrianised, tourists can enjoy an evening stroll or an early morning jog. Other aspects of the natural environment adding to Port de Pollença's appeal are the possibilities for cycling and walking, notably across the Cap de Formentor.

Furthering the appeal of Port de Pollença to families, there are also free outdoor play parks for young children on the corner of Méndez Núñez and Metge Llopis streets and further south by Citra de les Xarxes on the seafront (Figure 3.16).

A recent addition to Port de Pollença's built attractions is Fantasy World, an air-conditioned, two-storey activity facility with soft-play equipment in the town centre, 150 metres from the beach. The appeal

Figure 3.16
Port de Pollença

Key
- ✉ Post office
- *i* Tourist information centre
- ● Hotels referred to in the text
- ░ Sandy beach
- FW Fantasy World
- 🏛 Outdoor play park

Figure 3.17
Cafés on the promenade leading to Pine Walk

of this to parents with young children is that this is a holiday activity they do not need to join in with. At the main package holiday hotels, such as the Pollensa Park, activities for families are designed to keep customers on site so they spend more money, but some parents have felt marooned in the hotel and unable to enjoy the town as they would like. Fantasy World targets this market by offering parents the chance to relax with a drink or use an internet facility while their children are playing. If they prefer, they can use the Fantasy World childminding service and go out and explore the town.

Active tourists such as younger adults, teenagers and perhaps their parents may find sailing and water sports in the calm waters of the Badia de Pollença appealing. South of the marina in Port de Pollença there are travel and tourism organisations belonging to the support services sector that provide for a range of water sports including sailing, windsurfing, snorkelling and scuba diving. There are also sailing yachts available for charter, which appeal to older and more affluent tourists for relaxation away from the hot and busy shore in high summer.

Events

The annual fiesta in July features music outdoors and events for children including a children's party in the town's market square. Out-of-season events include the Pollença Fair in November, a religious procession at Easter that draws big crowds, and a number of smaller artistic and religious occasions. The summer fiesta appeals to the family target market of the resort, and the traditional Easter celebrations to older tourists who are staying in the resort out of season and want to see something of the traditional life of Mallorcan people.

Events are important to a resort to spread out the benefits of tourism. Local authorities encourage them as part of their destination management. Having the fiesta centred on the town centre draws families and their spending money into that part of the resort so that businesses away from the seafront gain more economic benefit. Out-of-season events keep tourists coming and spending at other times of the year.

Food, drink and entertainment

Seafront ice-cream counters, bars and restaurants line the shore from just south of the marina as far as the Pine Walk. Restaurant Stay and Pizzeria Tolo are two of the restaurants. There are more in and around the main market square and in a cluster close to the Hotel Pollensa Park. For self-catering tourists and those who want a change from the restaurant inside their package holiday hotel, these are part of the resort's appeal. Entertainment such as flamenco music and karaoke is offered in some of these catering establishments. Nightlife in the form of discos and clubs is not what Port de Pollença specialises in and, while the lack of them is part of the resort's family appeal, it may put off those younger, single tourists seeking a lively party scene.

Accommodation

Port de Pollença is not a high-rise resort, but there are some larger hotels used by package holiday tour operators such as Thomas Cook. The Hotel Pollensa Park is an example of this style of accommodation and operates on an all-inclusive basis with full board, evening disco and poolside games laid on. This suits many of the hotel's family clients, some of whom return year after year and spend much of their time in the hotel and its grounds.

Smaller hotels, such as the Hotel Miramar close to the Pine Walk, appeal to tourists who like a less structured approach to their holiday.

Hostel-style accommodation, such as the Hostal-residencia Borras in the town centre, appeals to younger, independent travellers who may have less money to spend.

Self-catering accommodation is also available. Direct Holidays is a direct-sale tour operator based in Glasgow and is part of the My Travel group. The organisation features the 3-star Oro Playa apartments in its brochure and on its website (**www.directholidays.co.uk**), which have their own private pool.

Evaluating appeal

The appeal of a destination for tourists varies from one type of customer to another. An approach to evaluating a destination by reference to different tourist types is shown in Chapter 3.2, where the appeal of New York City is considered. That approach can be applied to Port de Pollença or any other tourist destination.

Evaluating appeal also involves considering who would not find a destination, or elements of it, attractive. Port de Pollença is a family-orientated resort. Compared to other Mallorcan resorts, such as Palma Nova or neighbouring Alcudia, there is relatively little nightlife, so groups of younger, single people looking for a party destination would be well advised by a travel consultant to consider alternatives to Port de Pollença.

Time of year is also a factor when evaluating appeal. The peak season of July and August is hot and busy. The quieter shoulder season and cheaper out-of-season stays may suit senior citizens and other mature adult couples without children. Likewise, activities such as cycling and walking, to which the resort's hinterland is well suited, as well as sightseeing (in nearby Pollença, for example) may be more appealing to many physically active tourists when the weather is a little cooler.

Transport access

The travel and tourism industry provides transport for a UK tourist visiting a European destination in three phases:

- within the UK, from home to their exit gateway (airport, ferry port or Eurostar terminal)
- from the exit gateway in the UK to the entrance gateway for their destination
- from the entrance gateway to their final destination

In addition, transport may need to be provided for excursions from or travel around the destination.

Within the UK

Outbound tourists visiting Mallorca usually fly, although there are other options such as coach travel, rail and self-drive. In any event, the exit gateway needs to be accessed first.

The travel and tourism industry in the UK provides various options. Taking air travel as an example, secure airport car parking is provided by airport management companies and, in the vicinity of airports, by private car park operators such as Europark. Public transport access by coach and rail are further options. Some UK gateway airports have their own railway stations: Manchester, London Gatwick and London Stansted are three examples. Others like Newcastle International Airport have 'underground' access to the main city they serve. London Heathrow has a London Underground Piccadilly Line connection and the Heathrow Express train from Paddington Station. Taxis and self-drive car hire are other forms of transport provided by the industry.

Different tourists will choose different options for travel to the airport or other UK exit gateways. These depend on personal circumstances and preferences, although some are more likely for certain tourist groups than for others. Public transport is more likely to be favoured by younger adults without children, for example. Families with children may prefer self-drive options, parking at the airport. The degree of choice available also depends on where the tourist lives — some have easier access to coach and rail transport than others.

Between the UK and Mallorca

Most UK tourists fly to Mallorca. Table 3.2 lists airlines offering flights from the UK to Palma. This list changes from year to year and now features more budget airlines than in the past. Package holidays to Port de Pollença are organised by a range of tour operators including Thomas Cook and Direct Holidays. Package holidays include air flight and transfer from Palma Airport to Port de Pollença.

Options other than flying include a ferry service run by the Spanish ferry operator Flebasa to nearby Port d'Alcudia from Barcelona. Independent travellers can reach Barcelona from the UK by train, starting with the Eurostar to Paris, or by coach. Transmediterránea runs ferries to Palma from the Spanish mainland, with embarkation points at Barcelona, Valencia and Tarragona. It is possible to drive to one of the mainland ferry terminals either through France (usually at least a 2-day journey) or from Santander or Bilbao to which there are ferry services from the UK operated by Brittany Ferries and P&O respectively.

Table 3.2 Flights to Palma from the UK

Airline	Scheduled flights from
Excelairways	Birmingham, London Gatwick, Manchester and Newcastle
Monarch Selected Airlines	Manchester
Air Berlin	London Stansted
easyJet	Belfast, Bristol, Liverpool, London Gatwick, London Luton, London Stansted, Newcastle
British Midland	Belfast, Cardiff, Dublin, Edinburgh, Glasgow, Leeds Bradford, Nottingham East Midlands, London Heathrow and Manchester
Air Europa	London Gatwick
GB Airways	London Gatwick
Iberia	London Heathrow via Madrid
British Airways	London Heathrow via Madrid
Jet2	Leeds Bradford
Airline	**Charter flight from**
Thomson Flights	Over 20 UK airports
Thomsonfly	Bournemouth, Coventry and Robin Hood (Doncaster/Sheffield)
Air 2000	22 UK airports

Within Mallorca

The C713 road via Inca links Palma and its international gateway airport with Port de Pollença. Package holiday tour operators provide transfer buses for their clients. Long-distance buses run from Port de Pollença to Palma via Pollença and there is a summer service that runs from Alcudia through the resort to Port de Sóller along the mountainous C710 road. Car hire facilities are available at Palma Airport and independent travellers may book these in advance using the internet, for example.

Organised excursions

Boat taxis from the marina in the centre of the resort shuttle back and forth to the Platja de Formentor beach, half an hour away at the foot of the pine-covered slopes of the Cap de Formentor. Coach-based excursions are organised for package holiday tourists by tour operators. Local tour operators in Port de Pollença provide such excursions for independent travellers.

Recent trends and future popularity

The growth in budget airlines has helped make Mallorca even more accessible from the UK than before. There are more departures from regional airports offered by these airlines and by charter companies used by package tour operators (Table 3.2). Charter airlines also offer relatively low-cost seats for sale to independent travellers.

In the resort itself, recent developments have included enhanced water sports choices and the provision of support services like the Fantasy World children's play facility, providing for the resort's family target market.

It is likely that Port de Pollença will continue to be popular with UK family customers. Trends such as increased use of budget airlines and increased independent travel booked via the internet are likely to result in a reduction in the proportion of Port de Pollença's clients on traditional package holidays and a rising proportion of those making their own arrangements for accommodation, transfers and flights. Cheaper access to Mallorca from the UK will help bolster Port de Pollença's out-of-season trade among recently retired and **empty-nester** groups. Empty nesters are more mature adults whose own children have grown up and left home (hence the 'empty nest'). Such tourists may have travelled to Mallorca or even Port de Pollença with their children and now find a quieter time of year more appealing. The grown children of such visitors are less likely to visit Port de Pollença while they themselves remain childless. There is a relative lack of nightlife, and youthful tastes for adventure may encourage them to travel to other destinations — perhaps long haul. However, as the years progress they may return with their children to the resort they remember happily from their own childhood holidays.

> **Discussion point**
>
> What do you think will be the likely popularity of Mediterranean resorts such as Port de Pollença in the future?

Support your learning

Information sources

Information about Port de Pollença can be found in travel guidebooks such as the *Rough Guide to Mallorca and Menorca*; in tour operators' brochures and on their websites, e.g. **www.thomascook.com** and **www.thomson.co.uk**; and on resort-specific websites including **www.puertopollensa.com**.

Skills builder

Use an internet search engine to locate useful websites for investigating Port de Pollença and use travel guidebooks as printed sources. Compare the information you collect from different sources to confirm its accuracy.

Activities menu

Vocational scenario
Imagine you are a travel consultant in a travel agency.

a Propose three choices of accommodation available in Port de Pollença for a young adult couple, either as package holidaymakers or as independent travellers.
b Explain to a single and active senior citizen three elements of Port de Pollença's appeal that would meet their needs.
c Research and analyse travel options to Port Pollença for a family of four from your home area.
d Evaluate elements of Port de Pollença's appeal for meeting the needs of a family with a 5-year-old daughter and 15-year-old son.

3.2

Destination USA

Figure 3.18 shows the locations of some major tourist destinations in Canada and the USA visited by UK leisure and business tourists.

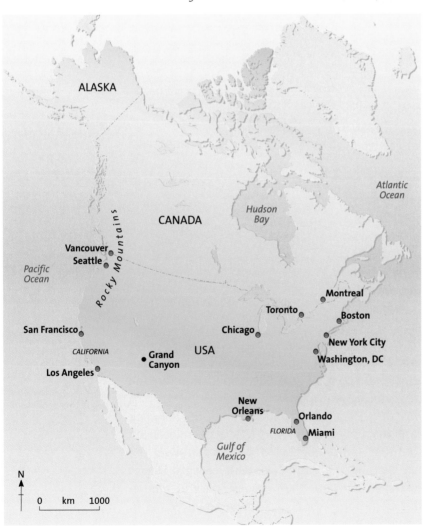

Figure 3.18 *Major tourist destinations in North America*

Case study: New York City

Location and landscape

New York City is located at the mouth of the Hudson River in southern New York State, which is in the northeast of the USA. Its location within North America is shown on Figure 3.18.

New York City is made up of five boroughs (Figure 3.19). Its central area, Manhattan, is an island in the Hudson River. The majority of UK tourists spend most of their stay on Manhattan Island. The Brooklyn Bridge is one of New York's numerous bridges that connects Manhattan to the mainland. To the west, the Hudson River forms the border with the neighbouring state of New Jersey. On the island's eastern flank, the so-called East River (actually a distributary of the Hudson) lies between the island and the boroughs of Brooklyn and Queens.

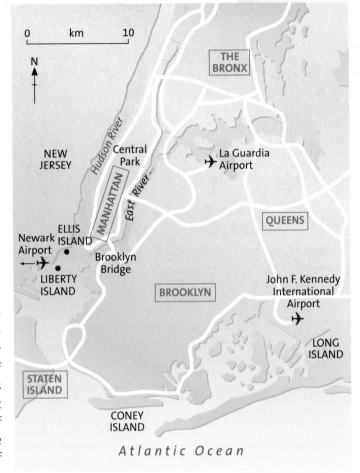

Figure 3.19
New York City

At the southern end of Manhattan, the large natural harbour of New York includes Ellis Island and Liberty Island, on which two of New York's principal tourist attractions stand — the Ellis Island Immigration Museum and the Statue of Liberty respectively.

With few exceptions, Manhattan is flat and very built-up. Being an island has long meant that building land on Manhattan has been expensive. At the southern end of the island and in midtown, the premiums were such that by the early twentieth century it was cheaper to build skyscrapers upwards than occupy space at ground level. The trademark Manhattan skyline — a major tourist draw in itself — was born (Figure 3.20).

©Comstock Images/Alamy

Figure 3.20 The
Manhattan skyline

Central Park is the only extensive area of open space in central Manhattan. Although parts of its landscape are natural — rock outcrops that were scoured by glacial ice — the park is an artificial creation, not a green wildscape remnant.

Climate

New York City climate data are given in Table 3.3. In the summer the city is hot and many UK tourists find it uncomfortably sticky and humid. Winters, by contrast, are very cold. New York does not benefit from the warming effect of the Gulf Stream/North Atlantic Drift ocean current like the UK does. In fact, the cold Labrador Current chills it and winters are harsh by UK standards. Climatically, the most appealing times to visit are spring, although it can be wet, and autumn.

Month	J	F	M	A	M	J	J	A	S	O	N	D
Minimum temperature (°C)	−3	−3	1	7	12	17	20	19	16	10	5	−1
Maximum temperature (°C)	3	4	9	16	22	27	29	25	25	19	12	6
Rainfall (cm)	8.6	8.4	10.4	10.7	11.2	9.4	11.2	10.2	9.9	9.1	11.4	9.9

Table 3.3 New York City climate data

Access

Travellers from the UK fly to New York via one of two gateway airports: John F. Kennedy (JFK) and Newark Airport, New Jersey. British and American airlines, as well as those of other countries, provide air services from an increasing range of regional airports in the UK as well as from London airports. Some UK tourists fly to New York indirectly from the UK, for example via Amsterdam's Schiphol Airport using the Dutch airline KLM.

Attraction	Nature of appeal
Statue of Liberty	• The icon of New York
Ellis Island	• Immigration Museum in the building through which European migrants to New York passed • Close to the Statue of Liberty
Brooklyn Bridge	• Free walkway affords spectacular views of the Manhattan skyline at night
Multicultural neighbourhoods, e.g. Little Italy, Chinatown, Harlem	• New York is a melting pot of many ethnicities • These neighbourhoods retain the essence of Italian, Chinese and African-American/Hispanic heritages
Villages, e.g. Greenwich Village and Soho	• Artistic and architectural heritage quarters
Central Park	• Large open space in New York • Carriage rides • The John Lennon 'Imagine' memorial at Strawberry Fields
Rockefeller Center	• Iconic building on 5th Avenue • Ice-skating in the winter months
Empire State Building	• For many years, the world's tallest building • Spectacular views from its observatory deck
Broadway and Times Square	• Theatreland and spectacular neon signs
Shops	• Bloomingdale's and Macy's are the main department stores • Designer shopping on 5th Avenue • Chain stores in the Manhattan Mall and alternative shops in the East Village
Museums and art galleries	• Museums include the American Museum of Natural History near Central Park • Art galleries include the Metropolitan Museum of Modern Art and the Guggenheim Museum

Table 3.4 New York's major tourist attractions

Most transatlantic flights leave the UK in the morning or afternoon, arriving in New York approximately 7 hours later. Return flights tend to be overnight, landing in the UK in the early morning after a late afternoon or evening departure from New York.

Transfers from airports

Organised groups of tourists use local tour operators' coaches to travel from Newark or JFK to central Manhattan. Relatively few UK tourists stay in one of New York's outer boroughs (Brooklyn, the Bronx, Staten Island or Queens). Individual travellers often use taxis for the 45-minute trip. Business travellers' companies may arrange limousine transfers.

Moving around New York City

The New York subway (underground railway) and the trademark yellow taxis are the principal means of transport used by tourists to move around the city, apart from walking. There is also a public bus network. Two of the major tourist attractions, the Statue of Liberty and the Ellis Island Immigration Museum, are on islands in New York harbour and can be reached by ferries that sail from Battery Park at Manhattan's southern tip. The Staten Island ferry links that borough to the rest of the city and affords good views of the Statue of Liberty.

Attractions

Table 3.4 summarises some major New York City tourist attractions.

Accommodation, eating and drinking

There is a great variety of hotel accommodation in New York City. Iconic hotels like the Waldorf-Astoria (Figure 3.21) and the Plaza are marketed to UK tourists alongside hotels belonging to major international hotel chains such as Marriott, Renaissance and Novotel.

Educational groups and younger adults especially may opt for cheaper hostel-style accommodation at one of Manhattan's YMCAs (Figure 3.22) or a hostel-hotel such as the Gershwin Hotel (Figure 3.23).

Figure 3.21 The Waldorf-Astoria Hotel

Vanderbilt Y

Vanderbilt YMCA is at:

224 East 47th Street
New York
NY 10017
USA

The nearest subway is a short walk away at Grand Central Station.

Rooms typically accommodate two and have a television but are not en suite. There are separate bathrooms and showers for male and female guests.

Room and continental breakfast. There is a diner/café on the ground floor where cheap but good and varied meals/coffee etc. can be purchased (e.g. breakfast) from 7 a.m. to 10 p.m.

There are also a swimming pool and fitness facilities.

Figure 3.22 The Vanderbilt Y YMCA

New York is a cosmopolitan city offering food and drink to appeal to every taste and to suit every budget from high-class restaurants on Park Avenue to street food on sale from carts on many of the street corners. Figure 3.24 is the advice given by a specialist educational tour operator to student customers.

Evaluating the appeal for different customer types

In Table 3.5, some elements of the appeal of New York City as a tourist destination for different customer types have been assigned scores between 1 (very low) and 5 (very high). A score of 2 represents appeal that is fairly low, 4 is fairly high and 3 is medium.

Gershwin Hotel

7 East 27th Street
New York
NY 10016
USA

Located close to the Flatiron building — New York's first true skyscraper. Private rooms are simply but stylishly designed. Dormitory rooms are rather more basic.

Diners and delis are close by in neighbouring streets. The Big Apple Diner is an authentic, inexpensive eatery.

Figure 3.23 The Gershwin Hotel

Figure 3.24 *Advice on what to eat and where in New York from a specialist educational tour operator*

Eat New York!

Of course, there are McDonald's and Burger Kings and the rest in New York — you are in the USA after all — but it would be good to try something a bit different, wouldn't it?

How to start?

- Ellen's Stardust Diner on Broadway is a retro-50s, authentic American Diner and a great intro to what you can get in the USA.

- Have a New York bagel with a filling like bacon at breakfast time, or try something more authentic like lox (smoked salmon and cream cheese). Ask for it 'to go' if you want the bagel wrapped to carry out.

- Buy a sandwich (pastrami on rye?) at a deli (there's a good one in Herald Square opposite Macy's) or take a booth at a diner. The Big Apple Diner two blocks uptown from the Flatiron building is a cheap and real diner experience.

- Breakfast — ask for your eggs in American: 'sunny-side up' (as we'd have fried eggs) or 'easy over' (turned for a little while).

- Buy street food like pretzels.

- In Chinatown, visit the Chinatown Ice Cream Factory on Bayard Street for an oriental flavour or two, maybe after a meal at the New York Noodle Town restaurant on the same street.

- Little Italy — past students have enjoyed good, cheap food including lasagne and pizza in Mulberry Street.

- Get some Harlem soul food — the cuisine of African America.

Recent trends and likely future popularity

Independent travel

Technological developments such as continued increases in booking travel using the internet have helped increase UK tourism to New York in recent years. Online bookers like Expedia and Travelocity have marketed their services in the mass media in order to involve an expanding proportion of the travelling public in online booking of independent travel with the facility of customising their own tailor-made trip of flights and hotel. Apart from convenience value, such an approach is often cheaper for the consumer and so more UK tourists have been visiting New York. There is no sign that this trend will not continue into the foreseeable future.

Built attractions	Customer type	Score	Comments
• Skyscrapers such as the Empire State Building and the Chrysler Building • Long, straight streets — 5th Avenue and 42nd Street are famous examples • Neighbourhoods such as Greenwich Village • Times Square • The Statue of Liberty and Ellis Island • Museums (e.g. the American Museum of Natural History) and art galleries (e.g. the Metropolitan Museum of Modern Art) • Chelsea Piers • Shops like Macy's, Bloomingdale's, the Manhattan Mall and 5th Avenue	Families with young children	3	• Famous landmarks and long, straight streets to walk along are not obvious attractions for this group. • Parents would need to make careful choices to keep the children happy.
	Families with teenage children	4	• These groups are more likely to have heard of the landmarks and want to see them. • They may also want to shop or visit the museums and the lights of Times Square.
	Groups of singles	4	
	Young adult couples	5	
	Large groups	4	
	Educational parties	5	
	Customers with special needs	4	• Some of the buildings have better access than others. • The Empire State Building is narrow at the top and can be claustrophobic as well as worrying for vertigo sufferers.
	Special interest customers	5	• People attracted by a special interest like art or the theatre have lots of choice and can base their whole holiday around their interest — visiting a different art gallery each day, for example.

Table 3.5 Evaluating New York's built attraction tourist appeal

At the same time, New York City has featured increasingly in the package tour operators' city breaks brochures as that market has expanded beyond the nearby cities of Europe to North African destinations such as Marrakech in Morocco and across the Atlantic to American cities such as Boston and New York. This move by the travel and tourism industry has placed New York in the minds of potential customers as a city-break destination they can aspire to visit in the less extreme temperatures of the spring and autumn seasons. Again, this trend seems set to continue, although the success of online booking is likely to result in an increasing proportion of independent travellers and a declining proportion of package tourists within this expanding market.

Air flights

There are plans to use larger aeroplanes on transatlantic routes, including those to New York. These superjumbos will increase the capacity of individual flights to carry passengers and, at least owing to short-term novelty value, will assist in the increased flow of tourists to New York City. Thereafter, they will be powerful tools at the disposal of the industry to ensure that there is continuing growth in the supply of services to meet the growing demand for tourism in New York.

Many return transatlantic flights (from New York to the UK) are overnight. This means that passengers are jetlagged after a relatively uncomfortable trip. This diminishes the capacity of business tourists to work immediately after their arrival in the UK. Airlines have recently attempted to tackle this problem. British Airways, for example, has introduced flat beds to allow passengers to stretch out and, it is hoped, sleep better. Such trends will need to continue in the twenty-first century as tourists expect increasing comfort and are less prepared to put up with twentieth-century-standard overnight flight conditions.

Other changes

The security situation in New York has affected tourist numbers in recent years. The terrorist attacks of 11 September 2001 on the World Trade Center (9/11) initially deterred some UK tourists from travelling to New York and it took a couple of years for visitor numbers to pick up. If similar events were to happen again, tourism would probably be affected once more. If not, continued growth can be expected as consumer confidence grows and remains high.

Since 9/11, security — especially at gateway airports — has become much tighter. This is uncomfortable for many UK tourists and has deterred a minority from wishing to return. However, it is not an impact that is affecting the general upward trend of visits to New York by British tourists. Tourists boarding the ferry for Liberty Island have their bags searched and pass through X-ray machines like those in airports. British people, however, are either used to this practice or tolerant of its need. It has not affected the general trend. Security is likely to remain tight in New York City but is unlikely to exert significant downward pressure on tourist numbers.

Changes in the exchange rate do result in fluctuations of tourist numbers. This is true of visits from the UK to any outbound destination. In 2004, the value of the dollar fell and tourists were able to get around $1.80 for their UK pound — this was more dollars per pound

Topfoto

Figure 3.25 *Fifth Avenue — when New York seems cheap, more shoppers are attracted to go there*

than just a couple of years previously. When New York seems cheap like this, more people are attracted to go. It is difficult to predict how the dollar will vary in the future. There is little immediate sign of it recovering substantially in the short term, so numbers of UK visitors to New York will continue to be buoyant.

Promotional activity by travel and tourism organisations has continued to encourage tourism to New York City. Tour operators and transport providers (airlines), in particular, have been active in the UK in promoting New York City as a desirable destination. The current trend of more flights to New York from more UK regional airports such as Bristol and Edinburgh, where the US company Continental Airlines has launched flights to Newark Airport, is making it easier for UK tourists to travel to New York. This is an important factor on the return leg of a trip when tourists are too tired to undertake a long journey home within the UK. Increased flights from regional airports are likely to make more people in rural areas of the UK consider a visit to New York.

Fashion also affects tourist numbers. There are fashions in travel and tourism demand, affecting the destinations that people want to visit. From the 1990s, the explosion in UK tourism to Prague, for example, was to an extent fuelled by a fashion for going there, and the same could be said of party tourism to Dublin. In the past, New York was always fashionable, with songs such as 'New York, New York' ('so good

they named it twice') and 'Lullaby of Broadway' being worldwide hits. New York City's high media profile has kept it fashionable for some time once it recovered from an image in the 1970s and 1980s of being a relatively dangerous place to visit. Television programmes such as *Friends* and *Sex in the City* in the 1990s and 2000s have continued to make New York a fashionable destination in recent years. The cinema, television, pop music and clothes design are all likely to ensure that New York maintains its status as a fashionable destination further into the twenty-first century.

Support your learning

Information sources

Information about New York City as a tourist destination can be found in travel guidebooks such as the *Rough Guide to New York City*, and in tour operators' brochures and on their websites. The NYC website at **www.nycvisit.com** is a useful starter to research on the internet. Websites of online booking agencies, such as Expedia at **www.expedia.co.uk**, are also avenues of enquiry to follow.

Skills builder

Use an internet search engine to locate useful websites for investigating New York City and use travel guidebooks as printed sources. Learn to be selective in the wide range of information you are likely to encounter. Compare the information you collect from different sources to confirm its accuracy.

Activities menu

1 Summarise the strength of the appeal of New York City as a destination for any one tourist type.

2 Suggest some places to eat in New York for a party of students on a budget who want to sample authentic New York atmosphere and food inexpensively.

3 Research and analyse travel options to New York City for a UK tourist from your home area.

4 *Vocational scenario*
   One the best known of New York City's hotels, the Plaza, on the southeast corner of Central Park just west of 5th Avenue, closed in April 2005 for 2 years for alterations. Imagine a trainee travel consultant was asked to propose some alternatives, in the same locality, for a client's 50th birthday party. He came up with these three options:
   a the Pierre Hotel, just east of Central Park
   b the Regency Hotel on Madison Avenue
   c the Chambers Hotel on 5th Avenue
   The customer was visiting New York with his wife and 11-year-old daughter. As the trainee's line manager, evaluate the recommendations he made.

Destination UK

The UK is a destination for both domestic tourists (people who normally live and work within a country and are travelling to another part of the country for a temporary visit) and inbound tourists (overseas visitors). The three main sets of reasons people visit the UK are for leisure purposes (including holidays), on business and to visit friends and relatives (VFR). Types of destinations within the UK are:

- cities, for example London and Edinburgh
- coastal areas and seaside resorts, for example the west coast of Scotland and Brighton
- countryside areas, for example the Cotswolds
- historic and cultural destinations, for example Bath and Stratford-upon-Avon
- purpose-built resorts, for example the Center Parcs Oasis resort at Whinfell Forest on the edge of the Lake District National Park

These types of destination overlap. York, for example, is both a city and a historic and cultural destination. Similarly, the Pembrokeshire Coast National Park in Wales is both a coastal and a countryside destination. Nevertheless, all destinations are clearly not the same, so it is useful to have a system of classification for them.

Case study: the Cotswolds

The Cotswolds is a countryside destination in England. The Cotswold Hills are a limestone ridge along which a long-distance path, the Cotswold Way, runs about 240 km from the market town of Chipping Campden in the northeast of the area to the historic and cultural destination of Bath in the southwest. Figure 3.25 locates the area.

The great tourist appeal of the Cotswolds is its landscape. The gentle hills provide a scenic backdrop to numerous pretty villages and towns. Buildings are traditionally made of the local limestone, which weathers to an attractive honey colour (Figure 3.26). Settlements such as Chipping Campden, Burford and Stow-on-the-Wold typify

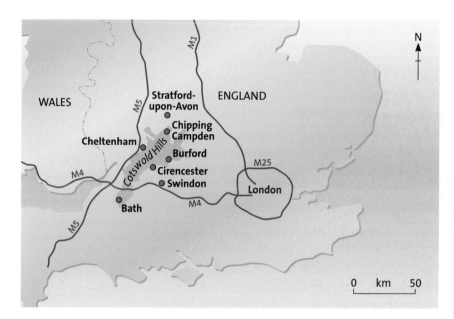

Figure 3.25
The location of the Cotswolds

'chocolate-box' rural England with picturesque stone-built thatched cottages, village greens with quaint shops and inns, and large country manors such as Sudeley Castle. Its image of quintessential Englishness gives it an appeal to inbound tourists that is heightened by the relative

Figure 3.26
Snowshill —
buildings in the
Cotswolds are
typically made of
local limestone

Gloucestershire Tourism

proximity of the Cotswolds to Stratford-upon-Avon (see Chapter 1.5), whose Shakespeare connections attract many foreign tourists north from London.

Unsurprisingly, the travel and tourism industry has been successful in marketing coach tours of the area. Some places, such as Bourton-on-the-Water, are honeypot sites and become very crowded with tourists, especially in the summer months. Away from these lower-lying places, the Cotswold Hills and the gentle valleys are much quieter and make attractive walking country that appeals to couples — the target market of the many inns and self-catering cottages that accommodation providers offer in the area.

Welcome meeting scenario

A tour company representative is accompanying a party of mostly middle-aged and recently retired American tourists, including couples and single people, on a 3-day coach tour to the Cotswolds. Some of the single people are in friendship groups. This is an optional excursion that represents an extension to the basic package holiday deal of flights to and from the USA, airport transfers and accommodation in a London hotel. Among the party is a family of a mother, grandmother and 8-year-old daughter. It is May.

Topfoto

Figure 3.27
Burford High Street

Introductions — I met most of you today — hope you all had a good day in Stratford — say who I am for rest of them and what I'm going to talk about now.

The hotel — hope everyone's settled in OK — any issues have a word with me at the end — health and safety — fire procedure — mealtimes on hotel leaflet (give out). Complimentary bar drinks after my talk, meal tonight in the hotel restaurant included in package.

Tomorrow (Day 2)

Morning: Burford

- Real Cotswolds. Really pretty town with lots of golden, honey-coloured Cotswold-stone cottages. Plenty of quaint little cafés. Shopping — antiques, souvenirs, clothes.
- Parish church — Norman but remodelled fifteenth century. American link — monument to Henry VIII's barber! (Edmund Harman) shows four Amazonian Indians — thought to be first time Native Americans depicted in UK (sixteenth century).
- Morning free for you to explore. Hill a little steep down to river but manageable. Ask me if concerned about it.

Afternoon: coach trip to Sudeley Castle

- Old English grand house. Beautiful gardens. Retreat of Tudor and Stuart kings and queens. Henry VIII's last (sixth) wife, Catherine Parr, outlived him — came to live here after his death when she married Lord of Sudeley.
- Paintings inside include works by Turner and Constable — two of England's most important artists. Gardens amazing. Queens Garden beautiful. Lovely spring weather now — just at their best.

Evening

Light nights now it's May. Ideas:

- Walk along the River Windrush banks through the hamlet of Widbrook — perfect little chapel there on site of Roman Villa (2000 years ago). Can go on to Swinbrook — really perfect English village — but 3 miles — probably not time unless late dinner, which I can arrange — don't need to do it all of course — got maps if required.
- English pubs — some lovely ones in Burford. Come with me at 6.30 p.m. to sit outside somewhere for drink before dinner.
- Dinner at hotel available — not included. See me and I'll make reservations. Angel Brasserie a good alternative in town. Can sit outside there if required.

Friday (Day 3)

Leaving Burford to go to Oxford en route to London at 11 a.m. — morning at leisure until then — after breakfast, chance to potter around shops — antiques? Presents? Friday, so May antiques fair on in Methodist Hall.

Questions? I'm always available — ask at reception if not around. Enjoy your stay! Time for a complimentary drink now, before dinner.

Figure 3.28 Welcome meeting notes

The tour company representative presents a welcome meeting to the party on the evening of their arrival at their hotel, which is in Burford, a Cotswold town on the A40 between Oxford and Cheltenham (Figure 3.27).

Day 1 of their trip has been spent in Stratford-upon-Avon and they will be staying here 2 nights before returning to London. Figure 3.28 shows the notes that the tour company rep uses to guide her during her presentation.

Support your learning

Information sources

Travel guidebooks such as the *Rough Guide to England*, the VisitBritain website (**www.visitbritain.com**) and the websites of regional and local tourist boards are potentially valuable sources. For Burford and the surrounding area the Oxfordshire Cotswolds website at **www.oxfordshirecotswolds.com** is useful, and for coach holidays to the Cotswolds the brochures and websites of coach operators are excellent research tools.

Skills builder

Presentation skills can be practised using the notes in Figure 3.28 to actually present the welcome meeting — see Activity 1.

Activities menu

1 Present the welcome meeting or write a fuller transcript aided by the notes in Figure 3.28.

2 *Vocational scenario*
   Imagine you are the tour operator's representative on the Cotswold tour. You have been asked by your line manager to suggest an extended programme for the next summer season. Outline your proposed itinerary for an extra day.

3 Research and analyse travel options to the Cotswolds for US tourists staying at a London hotel, other than joining a coach tour.

4 *Vocational scenario*
   Imagine you observe a junior colleague deliver the welcome meeting based on the notes in Figure 3.28. As her line manager, make notes for the evaluative feedback you will give her on the content of the meeting. You should consider:
   ■ both weaknesses and strengths
   ■ the extent to which the needs of all the party were likely to be met, including those of the family with the 8-year-old child

The welcome meeting

Roles of resort representatives

UK tour operators organising package holidays often employ resort representatives (Figure 3.29). Their job is to look after the welfare of the organisation's customers while they are in the resort. This is part of the customer service the tour operator provides. The quality of that service can help determine whether or not the customer decides to bring the tour operator repeat business.

Aspects of the resort representative role can include:
- greeting customers at the gateway airport
- accompanying customers on the transfer from the airport to their accommodation
- ensuring that customers are settled in their booked accommodation and resolving any issues that arise in line with company policy
- organising a welcome meeting for the organisation's tourist customers
- being available to customers as their contact with the tour operator and to deal with any issues that may arise, again in line with company policy
- organising and leading excursions
- organising activities such as a children's club or a beach barbecue
- accompanying customers on the transfer from their accommodation to the airport, supervising their successful check-in and bidding them farewell on the tour operator's behalf

Figure 3.29 *A resort representative*

Background to the welcome meeting

Aim

The aim of the welcome meeting is to settle customers securely into their holiday and destination so that they are equipped with the knowledge to enjoy their stay. Customers who have an enjoyable time are more likely to book with the tour operator again and are more likely to recommend the operator to other potential customers.

Elements

A welcome meeting should include the following elements:

- a formal welcome on behalf of the tour operating company and apologies for any delays, such as to the flight
- an introduction to the representative and any colleagues
- an accommodation briefing that covers emergency procedures, meal times, and facilities and activities on offer
- an outline of the destination's layout and main attractions
- advice on any interesting local events, such as festivals, that may be happening during the customers' stay
- appropriate advice on health, safety and security, e.g. sun protection, and precautions to take against any crime risk
- advice on local customs, such as when and where to cover up certain parts of the body in a destination with a different culture
- information about the services provided by the tour operator, such as a children's club
- optional extras — for example, excursions or a party night at a nearby beach bar (resort representatives may earn commission from the sales of tickets to such events, some of which may be initiatives of their own)
- details about how to contact the resort representative
- an invitation to hospitality provided by the tour operator such as complimentary drinks

A social event, such as a complimentary drinks reception, provides an ice-breaking opportunity as well as a first chance for customers to buy tickets for excursions and events that the representative has high-lighted in the welcome meeting. Such opportunities to 'close the sale' are important to the selling skills that the representative is providing to customers on behalf of the tour operator.

Figure 3.28 shows the notes used by a tour company representative delivering a welcome meeting to a coach party of inbound American tourists to the UK. Comparing these notes with the bullet points above provides a sense of the level of detail that might be expected. Welcome meeting scenarios also occur in domestic tourism and short-haul and long-haul outbound tourism situations. Groups of people arriving at accommodation in the UK, such as coach parties of UK residents, may also expect a welcome meeting to be provided.

Appropriateness

A resort representative may deliver similar welcome meetings on a weekly (sometimes twice-weekly) basis to new groups of customers. It is important that each group perceives the meeting to be fresh, as though they are the first to hear it or as though it is especially for them. Although they may have a standard set of notes or a script to follow, good resort representatives will ensure each welcome meeting's success by tailoring what is said according to the:

- audience
- location
- time of year

Within the same destination, all three of these variables need to be considered.

Audience

The content of the meeting should be adjusted to deal with the specific needs of different potential audiences. For example, in Port de Pollença (see case study in Chapter 3.1) in peak season, a tour operator's resort representative at a large hotel such as the Pollensa Park may be talking to a mixed audience, but one in which families are likely to be well represented as a customer type. Excursions, such as one to see the dolphin show at Palma Nova, and information about the children's club and nightly children's disco, are likely to feature strongly. Out of season, the audience may include a higher proportion of mature couples for which such information would be less appropriate. They may, however, be glad to hear of evening entertainments appropriate for their age group or of sightseeing tours that are available, perhaps to Palma or to the market in the neighbouring town of Pollença. An audience of sports enthusiasts or another of young, single people would have their own requirements for information to help them enjoy their holidays.

Location

Location is also a significant factor to consider in planning a successful welcome meeting. A resort representative addressing an audience in a city-centre hotel in Barcelona will have different messages to give compared to those delivered by a colleague in the nearby seaside resort of Santa Susanna, even though many of the seaside resort's customers intend to visit the city, perhaps several times, during their stay. Even in a smaller resort such as Port de Pollença in Mallorca, the representative may wish to include some details of what is available close to the hotel or apartment complex, such as local cafés and shops, and whether the beach opposite the hotel is safe and quieter than the beach in the resort centre.

Time of year

The time of year matters too. Mediterranean summers are hot, sunny and dry — that is part of the appeal — but sunburn is a risk and the tour operator will want to be sure that the representative has taken steps to ensure customers are aware of the need for protection. Events vary during the season — each week may bring differences. In Port de Pollença, there is a children's party in the main square during the July fiesta. Good customer service means that the resort representative makes the tour operators' customers aware of what is going on, and the welcome meeting is a good way to do this. The representative could mention the party specifically or, if there is a lot to say, draw the audience's attention to the fiesta and a list of events to be displayed in reception. Better still, there may be the possibility of booking places through the representative.

Delivery

The manner of delivery is partly dependent on the audience. In general, however, it is best to adopt an informal but efficient tone. The tourist audience is made up of people who are relaxing — even those on a business event are experiencing a change to the normal routine. On the other hand, the visitors are away from home in a place which is new to many of them. Reassurance is important in making customers feel confident so that they are able to enjoy their holiday. This is best achieved if they perceive the resort representative to be efficient and in command of destination (product) knowledge.

For particular customer groups, particular styles of delivery may be appropriate. One example is a holiday tailor-made for young adults. Expecting a week's holiday to be a week-long party, such customers do not appreciate a staid style of delivery at the welcome meeting. Something more fun is called for. Resort representatives need to have a particular aptitude to deliver a humorous, interactive style of welcome meeting, week after week.

Content	Appropriateness	Delivery
Elements to consider: • welcome and introduction • accommodation briefing • outline of the destination • local events • health, safety and security advice • advice on local customs • tour operator services and optional extras • contact details • hospitality	To: • Audience: types of customer present. • Location: centre or periphery of destination. • Time of year: weather, events.	Plan: • Style: vary according to audience type. • Length: long enough to put messages across; not so long that the audience is bored. • Time: early evening is a common but by no means obligatory time — it may depend on when the guests arrived.

A summary of factors to consider when planning a welcome meeting is given in Table 3.6.

Table 3.6 Factors to consider when planning a welcome meeting

Researching the destination

To present a welcome meeting well, the resort representative needs good product knowledge both of the accommodation to which the customers are being welcomed and of the destination. Table 3.7 summarises destination research methods.

Table 3.7 Researching destinations: a summary

Primary sources	Secondary sources
Visits Visit a destination yourself if you have the opportunity, and do research there first-hand by: • surveys and observation • interviews • questionnaires • secondary source collection	**Travel and destination information** • Tour operator brochures; other promotional materials (e.g. videos); websites (including online bookers). • Travel guidebooks and websites. • Destination promotional materials and websites. • Accommodation, transport and attraction support services' promotional materials and websites. • Media: travel features in the general and travel industry press, e.g. *Travel Trade Gazette*, *Travel Weekly*, *Insights*; television travel programmes; advertisements for destinations and providers. • *World Travel Guide* and travel atlases.
Witnesses Discuss the destination with travel professionals from: • travel agencies • tour operators • accommodation providers • tourist offices	**Statistical sources** • *Travel Trends* report on the National Statistics website at **www.statistics.gov.uk** • World Tourism Organization at **www.world-tourism.org** • International Passenger Survey on the National Statistics website at **www.statistics.gov.uk/ips** • National tourist offices and websites (search 'tourist arrivals' or 'passenger numbers' for visitor numbers) • VisitBritain at **www.visitbritain.com** • Statistics on Tourism and Research UK website at **www.staruk.org**

Evaluating welcoming meetings

In real-world situations, welcome meetings may be observed and evaluated by a resort representative's line manager as part of the rep's annual review and appraisal. Trainees may also have the opportunity to view welcome meetings delivered by more experienced colleagues, either live or on video.

Welcome to:	Presenter	
Accommodation _____		
Destination _____		
Date	Observer	

Element	Score 1 = very weak 5 = very strong	Comments
Welcome and introduction		
Accommodation briefing		
Outline of the destination		
Local events		
Health, safety and security advice		
Advice on local customs		
Tour operator services and optional extras		
Contact details		
Hospitality		

Appropriateness (to audience, location, time of year)	Delivery (style, length, time)
Observer comments	Observer comments
Presenter comments	Presenter comments

Figure 3.30 *Evaluating a welcome meeting*

As a travel and tourism student, practising welcome meeting delivery and receiving evaluation comments is a good way to build your skills. Your teacher and your fellow students, as audience members, are useful observers to provide you with feedback. A self-evaluation of your own performance in delivering welcome meetings is also valuable. This does not have to be delivering the whole meeting. You can write practice plans and deliver parts of a welcome meeting (such as the introduction, the accommodation briefing or the section that raises awareness of the destination's attractions).

You can also evaluate welcome meetings delivered by fellow students. If you have the opportunity to attend a real welcome meeting delivered by a professional, take it. Figure 3.30 suggests a method for evaluating a welcome meeting.

Support your learning

Information sources

As Table 3.7 shows, travel guidebooks, tour operator brochures and promotional materials, travel feature articles and programmes in the media and websites are all useful destination research sources. Tour operator training materials are valuable additional sources you may be able to access.

Skills builder

Plan and practise delivering sections of welcome meetings, building up to a whole presentation. Evaluate meetings delivered by you and others and act on feedback given to you to develop your skills.

Activities menu

1 *Vocational scenario*
   Imagine you are a tour operator's resort representative in Port de Pollença. Use the information given about the resort in Chapter 3.1 to write the script or a set of notes to support the section of a welcome meeting about the resort's attractions. The welcome meeting is for delivery to families with children who are staying in Port de Pollença in July.

2 Plan the accommodation brief section of a welcome meeting for one type of tourist staying at a named hotel at a particular time of year in a travel destination.

3 Research and analyse the out-of-season attractions available at a resort that caters for elderly customers. Present your findings in a format you could use to deliver the information as part of a welcome meeting.

4 Evaluate a welcome meeting you have observed, or self-evaluate one you deliver yourself.

Index